"Kudos to Michael Slote for advancing the boldest claim for an ethics of care and showing how it provides a superior account of both individual and political morality.

In this closely reasoned and far-seeing book, he argues for a Copernican revolution in moral philosophy, moving empathy and relationship from the periphery to the center of an ethical universe. In doing so, he exposes the heartlessness of patriarchal ideas and institutions that have marginalized caring and empathy along with women. Slote's reframing brings moral philosophy into alignment with current research in neurobiology and developmental psychology, revealing the link between reason and emotion, self and relationship, and showing the costs of severing these connections."

Carol Gilligan, author of In a Different Voice, *New York University, USA*

THE ETHICS OF CARE AND EMPATHY

In *The Ethics of Care and Empathy*, eminent moral philosopher Michael Slote argues that care ethics presents an important challenge to other ethical traditions and that a philosophically developed care ethics should, and can, offer its own comprehensive view of the whole of morality. Taking inspiration from British moral sentimentalism and drawing on recent psychological literature on empathy, he shows that the use of that notion allows care ethics to develop its own sentimentalist account of respect, autonomy, social justice, and deontology. Furthermore, he argues that care ethics gives a more persuasive account of these topics than theories offered by contemporary Kantian liberalism.

Michael Slote's use of the notion of empathy also allows him to provide care ethics with its first full-scale account of moral education, and he shows that the often-voiced suspicion that care ethics supports the *status quo* and is counterproductive to feminist goals is actually the very opposite of the truth. A care ethics that takes empathy seriously can say what is wrong with patriarchal ideas and institutions in a highly persuasive and forward-looking way.

The most philosophically rich and challenging exploration of the theory and practice of care to date, *The Ethics of Care and Empathy* also shows the manifold connections that can be drawn between philosophical issues and leading ideas in the fields of psychology, education, and women's studies.

Michael Slote (PhD, Harvard) is UST Professor of Ethics in the Philosophy Department, University of Miami. His areas of special interest are ethics, theory of rational choice, moral psychology, and, especially in recent years, political philosophy. Formerly Professor of Philosophy, chair of the Philosophy Department and a fellow at Trinity College, Dublin, he is a member of the Royal Irish Academy. He is also a past Tanner Lecturer and a past president of the American Society for Value Inquiry.

THE ETHICS OF CARE
AND EMPATHY

Michael Slote

 Routledge
Taylor & Francis Group

LONDON AND NEW YORK

First published 2007
by Routledge
2 Park Square, Milton Park, Abingdon, OX14 4RN

Simultaneously published in the USA and Canada
by Routledge
270 Madison Ave, New York, NY 10016

Routledge is an imprint of the Taylor & Francis Group, an informa business

Typeset in Goudy by Taylor & Francis Books
Printed and bound in Great Britain by
TJ International, Padstow, Cornwall

British Library Cataloguing in Publication Data
A catalogue record for this book is available from the British Library

Library of Congress Cataloging in Publication Data
Slote, Michael A.
The ethics of care and empathy / Michael Slote.
p. cm.
1. Caring. 2. Empathy. 3. Feminist ethics. I. Title.
BJ1475.S59 2007
177'.7–dc22
2007002635

ISBN 13: 978-0-415-77200-6 (hbk)
ISBN 13: 978-0-415-77201-3 (pbk)
ISBN 13: 978-0-203-94573-5 (ebk)

FOR JANE

[A] tension ... remains unresolved in this book: whether there is an endless counterpoint between two ways of speaking about human life and relationships, one grounded in connection and one in separation, or whether one framework for thinking about human life and relationships which has long been associated with development and with progress can give way to a new way of thinking that begins with the premise that we live not in separation but in relationship.

Carol Gilligan, 'Letter to Readers, 1993', *In a Different Voice*

CONTENTS

PREFACE

In recent years, the ethics of care has come to occupy a very visible place in ethical thought and theory, but most defenders of such an approach regard care ethics as a much-needed complement or corrective to other kinds of moral thinking, rather than as a self-standing view of the whole of morality. By contrast, this book argues that care ethics can and should offer a comprehensive account of both individual and political morality and that, conceived in such general terms, it is both inconsistent with, but also superior to, current forms of Kantian liberalism. (Along the way, I also indicate some reasons why I have reservations about consequentialism and neo-Aristotelian virtue ethics.)

I have been working on this project for many years – ever since I first heard of the possibility of approaching the abortion debate using the idea of empathy. There have been ups and downs, and one very large manuscript had to be discarded and then was eventually reworked as the basis for the present book. Even if what I am doing here is on the right track, I have left many issues for future consideration and elaboration; but I do think care ethicists can benefit at this point from seeing that their approach is more controversial, but also theoretically more promising than has generally been realized.

And the frequently voiced suspicion that care ethics confirms the *status quo* and is counterproductive to feminist goals is here shown to be the very opposite of the truth. A care ethics that takes empathy seriously and uses the notion systematically can say what is wrong with patriarchal ideas and institutions in a highly persuasive and forward-looking way. But, in addition, the idea of empathy serves as a general criterion for moral distinction-making in a way that has not previously been appreciated, and we shall also see how the recent psychology literature on empathy can help care ethics to develop the kind of systematic account of moral education that it has previously lacked. The ethics of care very much needs the notion of empathy, and that is what the title of this book is intended to convey.

ACKNOWLEDGEMENTS

Some parts of this book have been published previously in less developed and less expansive form. I would like to thank the editors of *Social Philosophy and Policy* for permission to make use of 'Autonomy and Empathy', which appeared in *Social Philosophy and Policy* 21 (1), 2004, 293–309. Material in Chapters 1–3 of the present book has appeared in several places: most recently in Rebecca L. Walker and Philip J. Ivanhoe, eds, *Working Virtue: Virtue Ethics and Contemporary Moral Problems*, New York: Oxford University Press, 2007.

I also want to acknowledge a number of debts to individuals. First and foremost, I am grateful to Tony Bruce for getting me to write this book at a point where, having earlier discarded a large manuscript in a neighboring area, I was unsure of how to proceed with my ideas. His encouragement and sagacity have meant a great deal. Many philosophers, psychologists, and educationists have given me helpful comments on one or another aspect of this book or the papers it derives from. Among them are: Kristin Borgwald, Michael Brady, Stephen Darwall, Nancy Eisenberg, Justin Frank, Carol Gilligan, Martin Hoffman, Thomas Hurka, Nel Noddings, Ellen Frankel Paul, Harvey Siegel, Allen Stairs, and Larry Temkin. I have an even larger debt to Susan Brison, Marilyn Friedman, Scott Gelfand, and two anonymous referees for Routledge, who read large portions or the whole of the present book in earlier draft form and who gave me trenchant and useful criticisms and suggestions at many points.

I have greatly enjoyed discussing the ideas of this book with my children, Cressida and Nathaniel, and, finally, I want especially to thank Jane, who has made all the difference.

INTRODUCTION

There has been a great deal of talk about caring in recent years, especially in the USA, where every politician says that he (or she) 'cares', and every hospital and medical insurance group claims to be 'the caring people'. In recent years there has also been a great deal of talk about how different men and women are in their approaches to just about everything – the oft-repeated bromide that 'men are from Mars; women are from Venus' is just one illustration of this tendency. I believe (though I can't *prove* it) that both these trends stem from one source: Carol Gilligan's seminal book *In a Different Voice: Psychological Theory and Women's Development*, which first appeared in 1982.[1] The idea that men and women are different is as old as the hills, but the specific claim that the way women treat moral problems is, on average, different from (but not inferior or superior to) the way men do was first enunciated by Gilligan.

I shall assume that the reader knows something about these developments and about their influence on ethics and ethical theory. Gilligan claimed, very roughly, that women tend to think of moral issues in terms of emotionally involved caring for others and connection *to* others, whereas most men see things in terms of autonomy *from* others and the just and rational application of rules or principles to problem situations. And one important result of Gilligan's work has been efforts to formulate and make use of an ethics of care or of caring that gives genuine expression to (what Gilligan said was) a point of view that is to be found more among women than among men.

The present book is one such effort, but it differs from most previous work on the ethics of care in some significant ways. First, it seeks to show that a care-ethical approach makes sense across the whole range of normative moral and political issues that philosophers have sought to deal with. This stands in contrast to what one finds, for example, in the earliest work that sought to articulate an ethics of caring, Nel Noddings's *Caring: A Feminine Approach to Ethics and Moral Education*.[2] Noddings made it clear that she thought our moral relations with distant people we have never met cannot be subsumed under an ethics of care, but must be understood, rather, in terms of such general notions as justice and rights.[3] And many of those who have subsequently worked on caring have similarly assumed that caring is only one side of morality, and that

1

traditional masculine thinking in terms of justice, autonomy, and rights also has some validity or proper influence within our total thinking about morality.

The present book, however, attempts to show that a care-ethical approach can be used to understand all of individual and political morality. To see this, we shall have to see how a care ethic can provide its own (plausible) take on justice, etc. When Gilligan drew a contrast between caring and connection, on the one hand, and justice, autonomy, and rights, on the other, she was referring to the way most men and most male philosophers have traditionally approached the latter three topics. But I think there is a distinctive 'caring' perspective on these topics, and I in fact believe, and shall attempt to show, that an ethics of caring can work for the whole of ethics or morality. Gilligan herself has at least suggested this latter possibility, and Noddings, in recent work, has also moved to some extent in this direction.[4] But I think I have pushed further in the direction of a unified total ethics of care than anyone else working on care or caring, and in fact most people now working on the ethics of care think of it as covering only a part of morality – though a highly important part and one that traditional philosophical thought, largely dominated by males, has unduly neglected. Let me say just a bit more about why I favor the more general or comprehensive approach, before I mention what I take to be the other most significant differences between the present book and other work on caring.

Most of those who don't regard caring as a total approach to ethics and political morality see an ethics of care as *complementing* traditional thinking in terms of justice, rights, etc. Or, perhaps better, they regard the latter as complementing the ethics of care. At any rate, such a view at the very least suggests that the two ways of thinking are compatible with one another: that they perhaps apply in or to different spheres of thought or different kinds of problems, but that they are not in open or deep conflict. In fact, several notable care ethicists – among them Virginia Held, Marilyn Friedman, and Annette Baier – have claimed that the two modes of thought are not only consistent with one another, but also capable of being *integrated* or *harmonized* within moral thought as a whole.[5]

However, the present book will seek to show that this is a mistake. To be sure, and as has often been noted, caring seems most readily applicable to personal relationships (the private sphere), and justice most relevant to public or political issues. But in later chapters I hope to show that caring and (traditional) justice deliver contradictory moral judgments about certain cases involving (supposed rights of) individual autonomy. So if we are looking for a consistent or integrated overall picture of individual and political morality, we seem to have to *choose between* caring and traditional justice, at least with respect to certain issues; and if, as I shall be arguing, an ethics of caring can develop a plausible view of justice (and autonomy and rights) all on its own, then that fact gives us reason to try to develop a caring account of all of morality, one plausible enough to give us reason to choose caring *over* (traditional) justice, when we deal with those issues where the two conflict, and more generally. (Of course, I am assuming here that care ethics and traditional justice-type ethics exhaust our available, realistic theoretical options.)

What also to some extent favors pursuing a more overall or systematic care-theoretical approach is the criticisms many have raised about Gilligan's methodology and conclusions in the studies she originally used to show that women and men approach moral issues differently. Gilligan and others have responded to these criticisms with further arguments and further studies,[6] but Gilligan herself seems to put somewhat less emphasis on male–female differences in some of her later work. (I shall explore the significance of this in Chapter 5.) Of course, anecdotal and personal experience to some extent certainly bears out or supports the (rather minimal) view that women, on average, think in terms of caring more than men do, but it is also worth remembering that the ethics of care is historically rooted in the moral sentimentalism of Shaftesbury, Hutcheson, Hume, and Adam Smith, all of whom were men. Moreover, the moral sentimentalist emphasis on benevolence itself shows the influence of the Christian ideal of *agape*, and the founder of Christianity was no woman. So historically, some important male thinkers have thought and/or written in terms congenial to an ethics of care. This fact, together with the questions that have been raised in the psychology literature about how definitely, deeply, or widely men and women differ in their approach to morality, should encourage us to think of a fully developed ethics of care as nothing less than a total or systematic *human* morality, one that may be able to give us a better understanding of the whole range of moral issues that concern both men and women than anything to be found in traditional ethical theories.[7]

The second major difference between this book and other work on caring relates to its philosophical character. Many of those who have written about caring and the ethics of care have been educationists and psychologists, rather than philosophers. For that very reason, they have brought expertise and issues to their discussions that philosophers can greatly benefit from; but I also think it is true that some of these writers, and even some of the philosophers who have written on caring, have been less worried about traditional philosophical positions and questions than philosophical ethicists not working on caring would tend to be. For example, there has been very little, if any, serious work by care ethicists on the nature and/or defense of deontology, a topic that is absolutely central to current ethical theory; and by the same token, care ethicists have had much too little to say about the nature and extent of our obligations to distant others, compared with those with whom we are intimate. (These same points can, I think, also be made about recent neo-Aristotelian virtue ethics.)

One of the present book's primary aims, by contrast, is to explore how an ethics of care can deal with traditional philosophical issues like those mentioned above. (Of course, to deal with a traditional question is not necessarily to come up with a traditional answer.) To be sure, there are many issues for which I don't have a (purported) answer – there are a number of topics the present book doesn't cover. But I will attempt to deal with several theoretical questions that are central to current-day (Kantian versus utilitarian) theorizing and that work on caring has largely neglected.

The ethics of care falls within (and is seen by its advocates as falling within) the ethical tradition known as moral sentimentalism. But the most famous of the eighteenth-century sentimentalists, David Hume, took on the full range of theoretical issues then known to the field of ethics. I believe the present incarnation of sentimentalism within the new tradition of caring ethics (Hume and the other sentimentalists never spoke about caring, only about bene-volence, compassion, sympathy) will achieve its greatest relevance to philoso-phy only by taking on the sorts of theoretical/normative issues it has tended to neglect.[8]

Finally, let me mention a third major way in which the present book will differ from previous work on the ethics of care. Care ethicists often speak about empathy and its role in caring attitudes and relationships, but they haven't stressed empathy to anything like the extent that I shall be doing here. I shall, for example, be making use of the recent literature of psychology to argue that empathy is the primary mechanism of caring, benevolence, compassion, etc. Though Hume largely anticipates this conclusion in the *Treatise of Human Nature*, care ethicists haven't really committed themselves to it in any explicit, theoretical way. Moreover, ethicists of care haven't provided a systematic account of moral education and development, of how moral dispositions are taught and acquired. But in the present book I shall follow the psychologist Martin Hoffman in arguing that a certain kind of (inducing of) empathy is central both to moral education and to moral development more generally. This is an idea that care ethicists are by and large unfamiliar with, but it will be central to the enterprise of the present book; and I hope one result will be to encourage care ethicists to pay more attention to the psychological literature on empathy and moral development than they have previously.[9] The present book's distinctive emphasis on empathy will also be visible in its systematic efforts to show that all, or almost all, the moral distinctions we intuitively or commonsensically want to make can be understood in terms of – or at least correlated with – distinctions of empathy. This turns out to have important implications for how an ethics of care can justify its moral claims across the entire range of individual and political morality, a theme I want to pick up again towards the end of this Introduction. But at this point I think it would be helpful if I gave the reader an outline of the rest of this book, chapter by chapter.

Chapter 1 introduces the primary notions of any ethics of caring. Such an ethics ties the moral evaluation of actions to caring as a motive/sentiment lying behind such actions and 'reaching out' to and connecting with particular individuals. But I argue, further, that caring motivation is based in and sus-tained by our human capacity for empathy with others. Chapter 1 sketches some principal findings of the psychology literature on empathy and moral development that bear on the moral issues any ethics of care needs to deal with; in doing so I also refer to the historical background of that literature in eighteenth-century moral sentimentalism. The chapter ends with an illustration of the connections among caring, empathy, and morality: the topic of abortion can be usefully illuminated, I think, by reference to those connections.

Chapter 2 moves on to a topic that I believe any reasonable contemporary normative ethics has to deal with – the issue of our obligations to distant people in other nations. Drawing upon the psychology literature discussed in Chapter 1, I argue that an ethics based on a connection between caring and empathy has appropriate means of criticizing, and perhaps even undermining, the approach to our obligations famously taken by Peter Singer in 'Famine, Affluence, and Morality'. *Pace* Singer, our obligation to help distant others is not *as strong* as what we have toward someone who is suffering or is in danger right in front of us, and this difference reflects a difference in normal empathic reactions. The relation between caring and empathy can also be used to clarify why our obligations to currently suffering or endangered people are stronger than those we have toward those who we know will suffer or be endangered in the future. But the literature of psychology also tells us that humans can and do develop substantial empathy for those we don't (now) see, so an ethics of care that makes a relation to empathy criterial to moral assessments in no way denies that we have substantial obligations to spatially or temporally distant others.

In Chapter 3, I discuss deontology and seek to show that deontological restrictions on helping others or ourselves can be understood and justified in empathic terms similar to those that operated in our discussion in Chapter 2 of our (less strong) obligations to distant or future others. Deontological restrictions on harming one person in order to help a number of other people are typically regarded as curbing or restraining natural human emotions such as benevolence and compassion. But if deontology and deontological moral reactions arise out of normal human empathy, then the assumption that we need to be ethical rationalists if we want to be able to allow for deontology is called into question. Rationalists already have a difficult time saying exactly why deontology is valid, but it is helpful to sentimentalist views like the ethics of caring if the latter *do* have resources for understanding the appeal of deontology.

Attention then turns, in Chapter 4, to an issue that is central to disagreements between Kantian liberals and defenders of the caring approach. Autonomy is an important, if not the most important, ideal in Kantian and liberal thinking about morality and politics, and it is not, at least on the face of it, obvious how an ethics of care can deal with this notion. Autonomy is an ideal with a wide and intuitive appeal, and treating autonomy as an ideal crucially involves the idea that it is morally incumbent on us to respect the autonomy of individuals. The ethics of care needs to say something convincing about the nature and moral significance of autonomy, and I believe the recent feminist literature, which stresses the relational character of autonomy, can be helpful to us here. The ethics of care needs to account for our obligation to respect – and not just to care about – other people; and it will turn out that the notions of empathy and of empathic caring are the key to understanding both our obligation to respect others(' autonomy) and the conditions under which autonomy itself, understood in relational terms, can be constituted and flourish. This will tie caring and autonomy more closely together than care ethics has ever previously attempted to do.

Chapter 5 continues the discussion of autonomy, referring to issues about when one may permissibly interfere with someone's freedom of action. Liberals think, for example, that one shouldn't ban or interfere with various forms of hate speech, but many feminists and care ethicists disagree, and this difference can, in the first instance, be accounted for in terms of the difference between the traditional liberal/Kantian conception of (respect for) autonomy and the more 'moderate' empathy-based conception that an ethics of care embodies. It turns out, however, that this theoretical disagreement doesn't correlate or correspond very well with gender (many women defend the right to give vent to hate speech); but in any event I shall be arguing that care ethics has a *better theoretical account* of the moral status of hate speech (and of other cases where the issue is whether it is all right to interfere with someone's freedom of action) than anything available to liberalism/Kantianism.

Chapter 5 concludes with a discussion of paternalism. Liberalism is, of course, wary of interference with people's freedom of action 'for their own good', but there may be reason for care ethics to be equally wary because of the great emphasis it places on connection with others. Some care ethicists hold that a caring relationship is less than ethically ideal if the caring isn't acknowledged or accepted by the person cared for. But, in addition, if there are no appropriate potential or conceivable circumstances in which the care would be acknowledged, *and the care-giver knows this*, then it might be argued that there is something morally questionable about what the care-giver as an individual is *doing*. Now when a parent takes an unwilling child to the doctor's, there is reason to believe the child will or would accept the parent's caring actions as an adult. Likewise, when we bestow care on a comatose patient, we can have reason to believe that the patient would be grateful if s/he only knew what we were doing. But if, for example, one knows that a motorcyclist, given his or her values, would never acknowledge or accept any intervention that prevented him or her from riding without a helmet, then intervening in this way might be thought inconsistent with good relationship and therefore impermissible as an action. So certain versions of the ethics of care may share liberalism's aversion to purely paternalistic interventions, while nonetheless disagreeing deeply with liberalism about the permissibility of interfering with people's freedom or autonomy in order to prevent serious harm to *third parties*. On the other hand, Chapter 5 points out other ways of developing care ethics that also lay stress on connection with others, but that end up disagreeing with liberalism (and with the aforementioned forms of care ethics) about the acceptability of paternalistic interventions.

But let me at this point dwell a bit on the implications of what I have just been saying about paternalism. The present book does not try to decide whether (a proper valuing of connection implies that) caring should be consistent with at least potential acceptance or acknowledgement. In that case, I am also not going to take a stand here on the related question of whether the value of caring relationships is ethically prior to the value of caring motivation – to caring as a virtue. This is something both Held and Noddings believe, and that I myself tend to disagree with, but the whole argument of this book is neutral on this question.[10] It is (therefore) also neutral on whether care ethics should be conceived as a form of virtue ethics.[11] But let me go on now to outline the remaining chapters of the book.

In the light of the discussion, in Chapters 4 and 5, of the nature and implications of a care-ethical approach to autonomy, Chapter 6 takes up the issue of social justice and defends a conception of that notion that takes sustenance from what has previously been said about the ethics of caring. Laws and social institutions can express or exhibit relevant empathically caring motivation, and this allows us to evaluate laws, institutions, and whole societies in care-ethical terms. I spend less time on the notion of rights because, as has often been pointed out, a conception of rights naturally follows out of any given theory of social justice. Of course, there are many moral issues, both individual and political, that our discussion here won't cover, but by the time we reach the end of Chapter 6, I hope it will be clear why I think it makes sense to think of the/an ethics of care as covering all, and not just some smaller part, of morality.

Chapter 7 seeks to draw the contrast between Kantian liberalism and the ethics of care in wider, and perhaps starker, terms. Kantian liberalism is a form of ethical rationalism, but the sentimentalist ethics of caring doesn't see immorality as a form of irrationality. The person who hates and hurts others, or who is indifferent to anyone but himself, doesn't necessarily seem to us irrational: what he does seem is *heartless*. Rationalists believe, and have claimed, that if ethical/moral imperatives aren't dictates of reason, morality ends up lacking the dignity, value, or force that it intuitively appears to have. But Chapter 7 argues that these consequences don't follow at all. It then goes on to discuss a topic that is a bit of a sore point in the history and theory of sentimentalism – the question whether there is any such thing as practical reason. Hume arguably held that there is not, but if sentimentalism defends such a view, it ends up denying the seemingly obvious fact, for example, that someone (roughly) who wills an end but lacks any intention of doing anything to further that end is a prime instance of irrationality (of a practical kind). So rather than remaining skeptical or nihilistic about practical reason, Chapter 7 instead attempts to demonstrate that an ethics of caring can actually account for practical rationality *along sentimentalist lines*. Concern for one's own welfare turns out to be the primary motive involved in practical rationality, and in that case means–end rationality and the rational avoidance of akrasia have to be understood by reference to that motive. This needn't, however, entail any basic conflict or inconsistency between being rational and being moral. In addition, caring relationships seem to be sustained by a mixture or blurring of altruistic and self-concerned motivations, and Chapter 7 concludes by considering how what has been said earlier about altruistic caring and about rational self-concern can be brought together in describing a/the care-ethical ideal of (building and sustaining) caring relationships.

The book's conclusion raises some important foundational issues. As mentioned above, I argue throughout this work that distinctions of empathy mark or correspond to plausible moral distinctions. As a general rule, what we find morally worse tends to go more against the flow of fully developed human empathy, and in every case discussed here, and that I know of, the actions we have reason to find morally acceptable don't indicate or exhibit a lack of human empathy. Given further (as I maintain) that empathy is essential to caring moral motivation, the broad correspondence between empathy and morality doesn't seem as if it can be an accident; and that is a reason for regarding facts about empathy or, better, empathic caring as justifying various (particular) moral claims. Or, to put matters slightly differently, it is a reason to treat empathic caring as criterial for morality across a wide range of individual and political issues. But it would be nice to be able to suggest some sort of explanation as to why empathy is relevant to right and wrong, and in the conclusion of this book I try to do this.

However, let me raise some final worries that need to be – and are – addressed in these pages. It is often said that an ethics of care is more appropriate to women than to men, and it is also frequently claimed that care ethics works against the goals of feminism by recommending the very attitudes and activities that have kept women subordinate to men throughout the ages. These two thoughts are in some tension with one another, but either of them could lead one to conclude that care ethics cannot function, or function well, as a morality governing both men and women. However, during the course of this book I hope to show that the present approach to care ethics doesn't have any of the above implications. We shall see, rather, that a fully elaborated ethics of care has the potential to function in a comprehensive and satisfying way as a truly human morality.

Notes

1 Carol Gilligan, *In a Different Voice: Psychological Theory and Women's Development*, Cambridge, MA: Harvard University Press, 1982.
2 Nel Noddings, *Caring: A Feminine Approach to Ethics and Moral Education*, Berkeley, CA: University of California Press, 1984.
3 This latter point came out more clearly in a talk Noddings gave to the Society for Women in Philosophy in 1988, published as 'A Response', *Hypatia* 5, 1990, pp. 120–26.

4 See Carol Gilligan, 'Letter to Readers, 1993' in later printings of *In a Different Voice*, pp. xxvi–xxvii (from which the epigram at the beginning of the present book is taken); and Nel Noddings, *Starting at Home: Caring and Social Policy*, Berkeley, CA: University of California Press, 2002. My own recent work has consistently defended the notion that an ethics of care can cover all of (individual and political) morality. See e.g. Michael Slote, *Morals from Motives*, New York: Oxford University Press, 2001; but the project was pursued in earlier papers as well.

5 See Virginia Held, 'The Ethics of Care' in David Copp, ed., *The Oxford Handbook of Ethical Theory*, New York: Oxford University Press, 2006, pp. 548f.; Marilyn Friedman, *What Are Friends For? Feminist Perspectives on Personal Relationships and Moral Theory*, Ithaca, NY: Cornell University Press, 1993, Chapter 5; and Annette Baier, 'The Need for More than Justice' in Virginia Held, ed., *Justice and Care: Essential Readings in Feminist Ethics*, Boulder, CO: Westview Press, 1995, esp. p. 57.

6 Gilligan cites (subsequent) studies that favor her 'different voices' hypothesis in 'Reply by Carol Gilligan', *Signs* 11, 1986, pp. 324–33. Among the many later studies that call her view at least partially into question are: Mary Brabeck, 'Moral Judgment: Theory and Research on Differences between Males and Females', *Developmental Review* 3, 1983, pp. 274–91; and Lawrence Walker, 'Sex Differences in the Development of Moral Reasoning', *Child Development* 55, 1986, pp. 511–21. (However, Gilligan cites articles that question Walker's conclusions in 'Reply'.) These papers are just the tip of the iceberg (of relevant publications).

7 Something like an ethics of care can also be found in African or 'Afrocentric' thought among both men and women. (See e.g. Patricia Hill Collins, 'The Social Construction of Black Feminist Thought' in Nancy Tuana and Rosemarie Tong, eds, *Feminism and Philosophy*, Boulder, CO: Westview Press, 1995, pp. 526–47.) In addition, there are very strong elements of care thinking in both Confucian and Buddhist thought, though this is not the place to discuss those connections. However, all these important examples of care thinking support the idea that the ethics of care can and should be regarded as a potential overall human morality, rather than as something just about, or at most only relevant to, women.

8 Hume's most significant defense of moral sentimentalism occurs in *A Treatise of Human Nature*, L. A. Selby-Bigge, ed., Oxford: Clarendon Press, 1958. For an important work that antedates the (official) emergence of care ethics, but that shows the strong influence of moral sentimentalism, see Lawrence Blum's *Friendship, Altruism and Morality*, London: Routledge & Kegan Paul, 1980.

9 In some work that we have done collaboratively, Nel Noddings and I refer to and make use of Martin Hoffman's views about inducing empathy (what he calls induction); and more recently (in Nel Noddings, *Educating Moral People: A Caring Alternative to Character Education*, New York: Teachers College Press, 2002) Noddings herself makes use of them. But I don't know of any other care ethicists who rely on the idea of induction.

10 See Virginia Held, 'The Ethics of Care', *op. cit.*, p. 551; and Nel Noddings, 'Caring as Relation and Virtue in Teaching' in Rebecca L. Walker and Philip J. Ivanhoe, eds, *Working Virtue: Virtue Ethics and Contemporary Moral Problems*, New York: Oxford University Press, 2007, pp. 41–60. My own argument against the priority of caring relationships can be found in Michael Slote, *Morals from Motives*, *op. cit.*, Ch. 1, and in an earlier paper cited therein.

11 Virginia Held ('The Ethics of Care', *op. cit.*, pp. 551f.) says that care ethics is definitely not a form of virtue ethics, but Nel Noddings in 'Caring as Relation and Virtue in Teaching' (*op. cit.*) seems to think it doesn't matter much whether care ethics is regarded as a form of virtue ethics.

1

CARING BASED IN EMPATHY

1. The Ethics of Care

Carol Gilligan's *In a Different Voice*[1] speaks of various characteristics associated with women's distinctive ethical voice, but doesn't very often mention the specific idea of an ethics of care or caring. However, in *Caring*[2] Nel Noddings not only mentions such an ethics, but attempts to spell out in detail its characteristics and commitments. (Although she thinks that an ethics of caring is distinctively feminine, she doesn't hold that men are incapable of thinking in such terms, or that they shouldn't be encouraged to do so.) Noddings was the first person to attempt to spell out an ethics of care, and I think it might be useful at this point if I were briefly to outline her (earlier) views and indicate some ways in which one might respond to them.

Noddings sees care ethics as requiring or recommending that individuals act caringly, and this means in effect that we act rightly or permissibly if our actions express or exhibit an attitude/motive of caring toward others. Noddings doesn't consider cases where our actions may exhibit neither a caring attitude nor its opposite – for example, the act of scratching one's head. But we can easily expand upon what she says if we distinguish between a caring attitude, on the one hand, and an attitude of indifference or hostility to others, on the other. An action is morally permissible, and even good, if it exhibits caring on the part of its agent, but in normal cases of scratching one's head, one's behavior expresses neither caring nor any attitude *contrary or opposed* to caring, and so what one does is morally all right but certainly not morally good or praiseworthy. Actions, on the other hand, that display indifference or malice toward (relevant) others count, ethically, as wrong or bad. There is more to be said in this connection, but the details needn't, I think, concern us right now. What does concern us at this point is how an attitude of caring or concern for others relates to those others.

According to Noddings, genuine acts of caring involve an emotional/motivational sensitivity to particular other people. One is concerned about the situation a given person is in, and one's focus is on the individual herself rather than on any abstract or general moral principles that someone might want to

10

consult in order to determine how to act toward that individual.[3] One may be simply and directly worried about how things in the situation and one's own actions may affect the welfare of the person one is, at the moment, concerned about, and the welfare of *other* people may be very much a background issue. In a given situation, this latter point may hold even for a utilitarian or consequentialist, but any ethics of care will be avowedly partialistic in a way that utilitarianism and consequentialism, more generally, decidedly are not.

Noddings says, for example, that we can have an attitude of caring toward people we know, but not toward people we are likely never to meet. But Virginia Held and I have argued that there is no good reason to limit the notion of caring in this way: one can have a caring attitude toward (groups of) people one is never going to be personally acquainted with, inasmuch as one is genuinely, altruistically concerned or worried about what happens to them.[4] Typically, what one is willing to do on behalf of people one merely knows *about* is less than one is, and should be, willing to do for those one knows personally and is intimate with, so there is a difference in strength between (the moral requirements of) humanitarian caring and (of what we can call) personal caring, but both sorts of caring are *naturally called* caring, and in more recent work Noddings herself has conceded this point.[5] This means that, as compared with consequentialism, an ethics or morality of caring is partialistic. It is also, according to the earlier Noddings, *incomplete*. If we can't have relations of caring with those we will never know personally, then our moral relations with them (the fact that it would be wrong to invade another country for reasons of national self-aggrandizement, or that it would be wrong not to help people in a distant country suffering from famine or an epidemic disease) are not governed by an ethic of caring, but rather by (largely) separate considerations of justice. However, once we acknowledge that our attitudes toward strangers or distant others can amount to caring (of some kind), the way is open to treating our relations with such people within an ethics of care and even, as I suggested in the Introduction, to understanding justice as a whole in terms of caring.

Noddings also lays great stress on the reciprocity involved in good relationships of caring. The caring relationship between a mother and a baby may not be a relationship of equal or mutual caring, but even a baby has ways of acknowledging the mother's loving solicitude – smiles, cooing, eagerness for the breast. Such responses are obviously gratifying to the care-giver, the mother, but Noddings thinks that caring *needs* to be completed in some kind of acknowledgement or acceptance of caring on the part of the one(s) cared for – that the mother's caring and the relationship between mother and child are ethically less satisfactory where there is no acknowledgement. In addition, she holds that we should not only be concerned about the wellbeing of those with whom we already stand in intimate, caring relationships, but should also try to extend the circle of such caring to include strangers and people we don't (yet) know. Her ethics of care recommends and/or requires the creation, building, and sustaining of caring relations or relationships.

11

Thus care ethics, on the whole, has been characterized by a concern not only for individual welfare but for good relationships. However, the present book concentrates mainly on the former issue. I am going to assume that specifically moral attitudes and obligations center around the desire to help (or not hurt) other individuals or groups of such; and I hope to show later that our concern to build and sustain (certain) relationships involves an ethical ideal that takes us beyond the usual distinction between egoism and altruism and thus transcends what is strictly or specifically moral.[6] I take up this issue more fully in Chapter 7, where I compare and contrast morality with self-interested rationality, but at this point we need to return to our outline of Noddings's views.

Noddings says that caring involves a 'displacement' of ordinary self-interest into unselfish concern for another person, and in *Caring* she also holds that someone who cares for another not only focuses on a particular individual, but is *engrossed* in that other person. That means, roughly, that someone who cares deeply or genuinely about someone else is open and receptive to the reality – the thoughts, desires, fears, etc. – of the other human being. When they act on behalf of (for the good of) the person they care about, they don't simply impose their own ideas about what is good in general, or what would be good for the individual cared about. Rather, they pay attention to, and are absorbed in, the way the other person structures the world and his or her relationship to the world – in the process of helping that person.

Noddings takes pains to distinguish engrossment from empathy, which she says involves a much less receptive and much more active attitude than engrossment. She sees the empathic individual as putting him- or herself into the shoes, into the position, of another person, and such (presumably voluntary) putting oneself into another constitutes a distinctively male way of doing things (think about it!) that stands in marked contrast with the more passive, or at least receptive and feminine, attitude she describes as engrossment. But here Noddings's usage is somewhat out of touch with the (then) recent psychological literature on empathy. What she calls empathy is actually just one kind of empathy studied by developmental psychologists, which they tend to call *projective* empathy. But as the psychologist Martin Hoffman points out in *Empathy and Moral Development*,[7] a book that usefully summarizes much of the literature in the field, there are other forms of empathy. And one of them, which he calls mediated associative empathy, involves precisely the receptive and, if you will, more feminine character that Noddings says is constitutive of engrossment.[8]

We don't, in fact, really need the term 'engrossment' in developing an ethics of care; we can talk of (the right sorts of) empathy, instead. But, more important still, empathy/engrossment plays a more determinative role in an ethics of care than Noddings or other caring ethicists have appreciated, and one of the main goals of the present book is to demonstrate this. The ethics of caring needs to pay more attention to the psychological literature on empathy than it has previously done, and in what follows I hope, at least in part, to explain why. Let me begin by saying a bit more about how psychologists conceive empathy and how they think it develops.

2. The Nature of Empathy

Before I introduce the literature of psychology, let me just make some preliminary remarks about what the term 'empathy' means. To begin with, the word itself didn't exist in English till the early twentieth century, when it entered the language as a translation of the German word *Einfuehlung*. That doesn't mean that the concept or idea of empathy was previously absent from our culture. Hume in *A Treatise of Human Nature* says important, groundbreaking things about what we would now call empathy, but he used the term 'sympathy' to refer to it, though the picture is muddied or obscured by the fact that he also uses the term to refer to sympathy (especially in the *Enquiry Concerning the Principles of Morals*). However, we nowadays have both terms and are constantly chattering about empathy, so it behooves us at this point to distinguish empathy from sympathy. In colloquial terms, we can perhaps do this most easily by considering the difference between (Bill Clinton's) feeling someone's pain and feeling *for* someone who is in pain. Any adult speaker of English will recognize that 'empathy' refers to the former phenomenon and 'sympathy' to the latter. (Shades of J. L. Austin's discussion of our intuitive understanding of the difference between 'by mistake' and 'by accident'.) Thus empathy involves having the feelings of another (involuntarily) aroused in ourselves, as when we see another person in pain. It is as if their pain invades us, and Hume speaks, in this connection, of the contagion between what one person feels and what another comes to feel. However, we can also feel sorry for, bad for, the person who is in pain and positively wish them well. This amounts, as we say, to sympathy for them, and it can happen even if we aren't feeling their pain. But perhaps an even better illustration of how sympathy can take place in the absence of empathy would be a situation where one felt *bad* for someone who was being humiliated, but in no way felt humiliated oneself.

The recent psychological literature contains many empirical studies of empathy and various discussions of the difference between empathy and sympathy (a small number of which run counter to what I have just been saying). That literature takes us far beyond what was known or available to Hume, but I don't propose to survey it here. I do, however, want to speak a bit about two books that themselves survey the recent psychological literature on empathy. C. D. Batson's *The Altruism Question*[9] and Martin Hoffman's *Empathy and Moral Development* both argue that various studies and experiments show that empathy plays a crucial enabling role in the development of genuinely altruistic concern or caring for others.

Batson considers what he calls 'the empathy–altruism hypothesis' in relation to a large literature that discusses whether (genuine) altruism is possible. The hypothesis says, in effect, that empathy is a crucial factor in determining

13

whether someone will feel and act altruistically toward someone in distress or in need; and one thing that seems to favor it is the fact that where people feel empathic distress in the presence of another person's distress, they very often act to relieve the other's distress rather than simply removing themselves from the scene and thus from the source of their own distress. Doing the latter would clearly indicate selfish or egoistic motivation, but Batson (much more than Hoffman) thinks that acting on behalf of the person originally in distress, rather than leaving the scene, might also be explainable in subtly egoistic terms. He spends a great deal of his book considering various studies and various ways of conceptualizing what goes on in the kind of situation just described, in order to see whether altruism is the most plausible explanation of the results that have been obtained in different studies and experiments; and in the end he concludes that the existence of genuine altruism and the empathy–altruism hypothesis are the most plausible hypotheses in this area. These conclusions are helpful, even indispensable, to an ethics of caring that assumes there is such a thing as genuine caring and that seeks to understand both the development of caring and various intuitive moral distinctions in terms of empathy. But it is Hoffman's book that offers us the clearer picture of how empathy actually develops and influences our capacity for caring; and his work also distinctively points the way toward a major conclusion of the present book – that distinctions of empathy and of *empathic* caring correspond better to common-sense moral distinctions than anything that can be understood by reference to caring taken, so to speak, on its own.

Hoffman argues that individual empathy develops through several stages, and that its connection with 'prosocial', altruistic, or moral motivations is more ambiguous or inchoate in the earlier stages of that development. A very young child (or even a newborn baby) can feel distress and start crying at the distress and crying of another child within hearing distance, and this operates via a kind of mimicry and seems like a form of 'contagion'. But as the child develops conceptual/linguistic skills, a richer history of personal experiences, and a fuller sense of the reality of others, a more 'mediated' form of empathy can be (involuntarily) aroused in response to situations or experiences that are not immediately present and are merely heard about, remembered, or read about. It also becomes possible for the (normal) child deliberately to adopt the point of view of other people and to see and feel things from their perspective. Although we sometimes speak of both these forms of later-developing empathy (and especially of the latter, *projective* type of empathy) as involving identification with the other, Hoffman and others insist that the identification isn't a total merging with or melting into the other: genuine and mature empathy doesn't deprive the empathic individual of her sense of being a different person from the person she empathizes with.[10]

Empathic identification, then, doesn't involve a felt loss of identity but, according to Hoffman, it does involve feelings or thoughts that are in some sense more 'appropriate' to the situation of the person(s) empathized with than to (the situation of) the person empathizing. And as an individual's cognitive sophistication and general experience increase, she becomes capable of more and more impressive or sophisticated 'feats' of empathy. Thus, at a certain point, empathy becomes capable of penetrating behind superficial appearances, and we may, for example, feel an acute empathic sadness on seeing a person we know to have terminal cancer boisterously enjoy himself in seeming or in actual ignorance of his own fatal condition. In general, as we become more aware of the future or hypothetical results of actions and events in the world, we learn to empathize not just with what a person is actually feeling, but with what they will feel or what they would feel, if we did certain things or certain things happened. Similarly, adolescents become aware of the existence of groups or classes of people and the common goals or interests that may unite them, and this makes empathy with the plight, say, of the homeless or the challenged or various oppressed races, nations, or ethnicities possible and real for adolescents in a way that would not have been possible earlier in their lives.

Finally, Hoffman holds that the development of full moral motivation and behavior requires the intervention of parents and others making use of what he calls 'inductive discipline' or, simply, 'induction'. Induction contrasts with the 'power-asserting' attempt to discipline or train a child through sheer threats (carried out if the child doesn't comply) and with attempts to inculcate moral thought, motivation, and behavior (merely) by citing, or admonishing with, explicit moral rules or precepts. Inductive training depends, rather, on the child's capacity for empathy with others and involves someone's noticing when a child hurts others and then making the child vividly aware of the harm that he or she has done – most notably by making the child imagine how it would feel to experience similar harm. This leads the child (with a normal capacity for empathy) to feel bad about what s/he has done. Hoffman believes that if such training is applied consistently over time, the child will come to associate bad feelings (guilt) with situations in which the harm s/he can do is not yet done, an association that is functionally autonomous of parents' or others' actual intervention and constitutes or supports altruistic motivation.[11] He calls such habitual associations 'scripts', and holds that they underlie and power (the use of) moral principles or rules that objectify (my term) that association in claims like 'hurting people is wrong'.

In what follows, I shall assume what Batson and Hoffman have argued for on the basis of recent studies and experiments, namely that empathy is a crucial source and sustainer of altruistic concern or caring about (the wellbeing of) others. In particular, differences in strength or force of empathy make a difference to how much we care about the fate of others in various different situations, and this is something that Hume's genius was capable of understanding, even in the absence of empirical social–scientific research. But I need now to be more specific about how these and other findings and speculations can be brought to bear on issues of morality and shown to be relevant, in particular, to the ethics of care.

I believe that empathy and the notion of empathic caring for or about others offer us a plausible criterion of moral evaluation. Differences in (the strength of) normally or fully developed human empathy correspond pretty well, I think, to differences of intuitive moral evaluation, and that fact (if I can demonstrate that it is one) will allow an ethics of caring that brings in empathy – an ethics of empathic caring – to give a fairly general account of both public/political and private/individual morality. (I shall not assume that public and private are exclusive or mutually irrelevant domains – quite the contrary.) Let me begin by illustrating these themes with reference to the example that got me started on empathy, that made me feel that I had to go beyond mere caring to the idea of empathic caring. The example is a dangerously controversial one, however: the issue of the morality of abortion. What I have to say is really just preliminary and tentative. It is certainly less fully worked out than what I want to say in coming chapters about our obligations to help other people and about deontological restrictions on when or how we can help them. However, the application of the idea of empathy to moral issues is nicely and simply illustrated by the case of abortion, so let me jump in.

3. Empathy and the Morality of Abortion

Many discussions of the morality of abortion focus, roughly, on whether a woman has a right to choose an abortion and/or on whether the fetus, embryo, or zygote is a human being or person with rights. But in recent years other ways of approaching the morality of abortion have come into view. Thus in her influential article, 'Virtue Theory and Abortion', Rosalind Hursthouse treats the issue of whether fetuses have rights and of whether women have rights as secondary to the moral issues surrounding abortion.[12] She holds that something valuable is lost when an abortion occurs (though she doesn't say a great deal about this), and even if she may be willing to grant that women in some sense have a right to abort, I don't believe she would think this closes the issue of whether given acts of abortion are morally right. For the right of women to abort may be a matter of what others and, in particular, the state may or may not permissibly do to prevent a woman's obtaining an abortion, but even granting that the state may not interfere, the woman herself and/or a doctor performing the abortion may act wrongly, according to Hursthouse, because their actions exemplify or display a vicious or bad motive.[13] If a woman obtains an abortion because she (reasonably) thinks she is too poor, or in too poor health, to take good care of a(nother) child, that is one thing, and it respects, Hursthouse thinks, the value of the fetus. But if a woman is rich and frivolously decides that she can't be bothered taking care of a baby, then according to Hursthouse she may display a light-mindedness, a lack of seriousness about the values involved, that amounts to a vice. Similarly, to use an example of my own, if a woman has an abortion *solely* in order to spite her husband, who very much wants a child, we may think she is acting very wrongly, even though we may also be willing to grant that the state – or even, perhaps, her husband – has no moral right to intervene.

Understood from this new angle, the rightness or wrongness of abortion decisions is not a matter of conformity to independently existing human/political rights or moral rules, but derives instead from the character or motivation that lies behind such decisions. Hursthouse's arguments and conclusions seek to refocus our moral attention *vis-à-vis* abortion, and I think an ethics of care can quite naturally agree with her that the moral questions surrounding abortion depend, in the first instance, not on rights but on underlying motivation and character. But Hursthouse is a neo-Aristotelian virtue ethicist, and her approach makes no appeal to distinctions regarding empathy. However, the ethics of caring falls clearly within the Humean moral-sentimentalist tradition, and I hope now to make it clear why such an ethics might want to appeal to empathy in taking some initial steps toward clarifying the moral issues surrounding abortion.

Though some care ethicists discuss the morality of abortion[14] and many make use of the idea of empathy, I don't believe any other care ethicist has used the notion of empathy in talking about abortion. In fact, the only person I know of who has relied on empathy in this connection is the Catholic thinker (and US appellate judge) John Noonan, in an undeservedly neglected article entitled 'Responding to Persons: Methods of Moral Argument in Debate over Abortion'.[15] Noonan takes us beyond the usual questions concerning the rights of the fetus by asking us to consider how the idea of empathy with the fetus bears on the morality of abortion and, in particular, on the rights of the fetus.

He says that the notion of '[v]icarious experience appears strained to the outer limit when one is asked to consider the experience of the fetus. No one remembers being born, no one knows what it is like to die. Empathy may, however, supply for memory, as it does in other instances when we refer to the experience of infants who cannot speak or to the experience of death by those who cannot speak again. The experience of the fetus is no more beyond our knowledge than the experience of the baby and the experience of dying' (p. 303). Noonan argues, in effect, that we can empathize/sympathize with the fetus and that when we do so, we find the fetus to be 'within the family of man'. We accept, that is, its right to life.

However, what immediately struck me, when I started thinking about this article, was what a two-edged sword the idea of empathy can be within the abortion context. Yes, if the experience of the fetus is no more beyond our knowledge than that of the newborn baby and if we empathize equally with them both, then we may well feel, with Noonan, that they ought to be treated the same (and that abortions are morally wrong). But *are* their experiences equally accessible to us? Do we, or can we, really empathize as much with a fetus as with a (born) baby? It seems to me that there is reason to think not, and in that case the highly original notion of invoking empathy within the abortion debate may actually support some of the views of those who advocate a woman's 'right to choose'.[16]

Noonan argues that the principal task of defenders of the fetus is to make the fetus visible, a task different only in degree from that assumed by defenders of others who have been or are overlooked – for example, people 'out of sight' in prisons or mental hospitals, as well as blacks and other minorities. However, even if we can make, and have made, the fetus literally visible through photographs and films and even television in a way not possible in earlier eras, it is not clear that this bears univocally on the question of empathy. (The same holds for fetuses preserved in jars and displayed at pro-life rallies or demonstrations.) Very early fetuses and embryos look more like fish or salamanders or (at least) non-human, lower animals than like human beings, and they lack experience, a brain, and even limbs. All this makes embryos and early-stage fetuses seem alien to us and helps to explain why in fact (given relevant information and perceptual data) we naturally tend to empathize *more* with the later stages than with the earlier.

This point, however, is one that Noonan never considers, and when one does take it into account, then a caring morality that takes empathy seriously is given some reason to claim that it is morally better, or less bad, to abort an embryo or early-stage fetus than to abort a late-stage fetus. For the latter act goes more (strongly) against the flow of developed human empathy than does the former act, and we can use that difference as a justification for saying that aborting a late-stage fetus is morally worse or more unacceptable than aborting an early-stage fetus or embryo. So, *pace* Noonan, our appeal to empathy here, far from showing the wrongness of abortion, allows us to draw a conclusion that seems congenial not only to many opponents but also to *many defenders* of the right to choose. But if late-stage fetuses are easier to empathize with than early-stage fetuses or embryos, can we make a similar distinction between babies and (late-stage) fetuses?

It would seem perhaps that we cannot. After all, a late-stage fetus may be viable and about to be born, and it may be more mature or developed than some babies who have already been born. So shouldn't we readily empathize equally with neonates and relevantly mature late-stage fetuses? I'm not sure.

First of all, even if we make the fetus visible and even audible through films, photographs, sonograms, and television cameras, such means of perceptual or quasi-perceptual contact or connection are, at best, indirect. To put the matter in terms that will come into greater focus in Chapter 2, such contact with the fetus is less *immediate* than what we have with even a new-born baby. The new-born child is there, right in front of us, and we can hold her or look her in the eye, and such factors (as Chapter 2 should help to make even clearer) make empathy much easier than what we can experience, with occasional help from television, etc., with regard to a fetus, embryo, or zygote. There is also the fact that babies *cry*. Perhaps because it reminds us of our own vulnerability, but probably for various other reasons as well, crying pulls at our heartstrings and makes a baby seem one of us, or one with us. It calls out to us and touches us in a distinctive way (despite the fact that loud crying can at the same time be abrasive and annoying); and if this is so, then I think we can conclude that crying helps evoke empathic reactions in a way that has no parallel in what a fetus or embryo may do to affect us.

In that case, once again, the fact that killing a newborn goes more strongly against the flow or tendencies of normal human empathy than does aborting a fetus or embryo can be taken, by an ethics of care, as indicating the greater wrongness or lesser moral acceptability of killing the newborn. But of course none of this proves that it is morally all right or permissible to abort a fetus or embryo. I think an argument similar to the above might be developed in that direction, but the complications involved are, as I see them, daunting. I prefer at this juncture to move on to another (and less contentious) moral topic, but I believe our previous discussion at least helps us to see how differences of empathy can be used to clarify moral issues about what is intuitively better or more acceptable and what is intuitively worse or less acceptable. I would like now to apply these methods to the question of our moral obligations to help others, and we shall see that a care ethics that makes criterial use of the idea of empathy can make a good deal of headway on that question.

One final point. The reader may wonder whether a methodology of appealing to empathy can be used to understand better our obligations to animals. But I have found this question to be even more complicated and daunting than the issues that arise in connection with abortion. (I hope to pursue both these topics at a later time.) It is also worth noting that caring (about) can be understood broadly enough to take in not merely animals, fetuses, and people, but also ideas and ideals. It is not at all clear, though, that the latter are appropriate objects of moral concern, and certainly it is difficult to make sense of empathy with abstract objects. So I take it that an ethics of care doesn't have to, or want to, worry about this broader sense or kind of caring. On the other hand, caring about and even empathy with plants, the environment, and the biosphere may not be *completely* out of the question; but once again I propose to limit the rest of the present project to discussing care and empathy directed at, or responsive to, people or groups of people.

Notes

1 Carol Gilligan, *In a Different Voice: Psychological Theory and Women's Development*, Cambridge, MA: Harvard University Press, 1982.
2 Nel Noddings, *Caring: A Feminine Approach to Ethics and Moral Education*, Berkeley, CA: University of California Press, 1984.
3 Similar points are made by Carol Gilligan, *In a Different Voice*, op. cit. Note too that the ethical theory of caring to be developed here won't propose itself as something that needs to be thought about or considered by caring individuals in their relations with other people. That would be entirely out of keeping with what the care ethicist thinks about the high value of directly focusing on (the welfare of) other people. The same point holds for the general criterion of right action to be offered in Chapter 2 – as our discussion, in Chapter 5, of Bernard Williams's 'one thought too many' argument should make especially clear.

4 See Virginia Held, *Feminist Morality: Transforming Culture, Society, and Politics*, Chicago, IL: University of Chicago Press, 1993, p. 223; and Michael Slote, 'Agent-Based Virtue Ethics', *Midwest Studies in Philosophy* 20, 1995, pp. 97, 101.

5 See Nel Noddings, *Starting at Home: Caring and Social Policy*, Berkeley, CA: University of California Press, esp. pp. 21–24.

6 Virginia Held takes something like this view of the building/sustaining of relationships in 'The Ethics of Care' in David Copp., ed., *The Oxford Handbook of Ethical Theory*, New York: Oxford University Press, 2006, p. 540. My own discussion is greatly indebted to hers.

7 Martin L. Hoffman, *Empathy and Moral Development: Implications for Caring and Justice*, Cambridge: Cambridge University Press, 2000.

8 Martin L. Hoffman, *ibid.*, pp. 49–62. I should mention that Noddings has recently made it very clear she is aware that the literature of psychology describes and discusses a kind of empathy that closely resembles what she calls engrossment. See Nel Noddings, *Educating Moral People: A Caring Alternative to Character Education*, New York: Teachers College Press, 2002, p. 151. For relevant discussion of different kinds of empathy, see Justin D'Arms, 'Empathy and Evaluative Inquiry', *Chicago Kent Law Review* 74, 2000, pp. 1489ff.

9 C. D. Batson, *The Altruism Question: Toward a Social–Psychological Answer*, Hillsdale, NJ: Lawrence Erlbaum Associates, 1991.

10 On this point see Martin Hoffman, *Empathy and Moral Development*, op. cit., pp. 276ff.; *passim*. Similar ideas are to be found in John Deigh, 'Empathy and Universalizability' in L. May, M. Friedman and A. Clark, eds, *Mind and Morals*, Cambridge, MA: Bradford (MIT), 1996, pp. 213f. Deigh borrows from Max Scheler, *The Nature of Sympathy*, Hamden, CT: Shoestring Press, 1970, pp. 8–36.

11 Hoffman thinks power assertion and admonition inevitably play a role in parental discipline, but holds that a preponderant use of inductive discipline is more likely to bring about individuals with moral, altruistic, caring motivation. For discussion of some of the evidence that favors this view, see Mark Davis, *Empathy: A Social Psychological Approach*, Madison, WI: Brown & Benchmark, 1994, pp. 70ff.; and Nancy Eisenberg, *The Caring Child*, Cambridge, MA: Harvard University Press, 1992.

12 Rosalind Hursthouse, 'Virtue Theory and Abortion', *Philosophy and Public Affairs* 20, 1991, pp. 223–46.

13 Others have distinguished between the right to abortion and the morality of abortion without relying on any sort of virtue-ethical approach to its morality.

14 See e.g. Nel Noddings, *Starting at Home*, op. cit., pp. 235–37.

15 John Noonan, 'Responding to Persons: Methods of Moral Argument in Debate over Abortion', *Theology Digest*, 1973, pp. 291–307. I am indebted to Allen Stairs for bringing this article to my attention.

16 In speaking of the right to choose here, I am speaking of what it is right for an individual to do, not of what it is right or obligatory for a society or state to permit – although the phrase 'right to choose' is typically used to refer to the latter issue.

2

OUR OBLIGATIONS TO HELP OTHERS

I have said that care ethics treats acts as right or wrong, depending on whether they exhibit a caring or uncaring attitude/motivation on the part of the agent. But surely this formula needs clarification and expansion. A single act may show an empathically caring attitude toward some people, and a lack of empathic caring, even malice, toward others. So an ethics of caring needs to be able to say how a caring individual relates to all the different people she knows or (merely) knows about. We shall take up this challenge in the present chapter and do so, again, by reference to empathy and distinctions of empathy.

1. Immediacy and Distance

I believe the best way to show that the ethics of empathic caring (as we can call the present approach) can give us a plausible general account of our obligations to help others, is to begin with a discussion of Peter Singer's classic article 'Famine, Affluence, and Morality'.[1] In that article Singer argues that our obligations to distant and personally unknown others are just as strong as those we have to those who are near and/or known to us. Thus if a child is drowning right in front of one, and one can easily save her, it would normally be morally wrong not to do so, and almost everyone is willing to agree that we are morally obligated here. But most people think we are not similarly (or as strongly) obligated to save the life of a distant child by making, say, a small contribution to Oxfam; yet, as Singer points out in his article, the most *obvious* difference between the drowning child and children we can save via contributions to Oxfam is one of spatial distance.

Singer thinks it is pretty clear that sheer distance cannot be morally relevant to our obligations to aid and, as a result, he concludes that we are just as obligated to give to Oxfam as to save the drowning child. But in recent years his quick dismissal of distance has come to be questioned on the basis of considerations that I want to examine here while, at the same time, arguing that empathy in fact gives a firmer basis than distance for distinguishing the strength of our obligation to the drowning child and our obligations to those we can only help (say) through organizations like Oxfam. Spatial distance and (decreasing) empathy do in fact correlate with one another across a wide range of cases, and that very fact may have helped to obscure the role empathy potentially has in explaining the sorts of distinctions people intuitively, or commonsensically, want to make with regard to the kinds of cases Singer mentions. But before saying anything more about the role of empathy here, it will be useful to say a bit more about the role sheer spatial distance might be thought to play in Singer-like cases.

Some of those who have lately considered the moral relevance of distance have regarded that issue as effectively involving two separate questions: first, whether we intuitively regard distance as making a difference to our obligations, and second, whether different intuitive reactions to third- or first-person cases involving distance would show anything important about (differences in) our actual obligations. In his book *Living High and Letting Die*, for example, Peter Unger considers both these issues and defends a negative answer to both of them. He thinks our superficial intuitions about cases may not ultimately carry much weight in moral theory or in determining where our obligations really lie. But he also holds that our differing moral intuitions about relevant cases don't track distance so much as (what he calls) salience and conspicuousness.[2]

However, Frances Kamm disagrees with these views. She thinks that (a rather complicated notion of) distance *does* help to explain our differing intuitions about cases, and also is relevant to our actual obligations in such cases.[3] Singer asks us to consider the difference between a situation where we can save a child from drowning at small cost to ourselves and one where we can save a distant child from starvation by making a small contribution to a famine relief organization, noting, but also deploring, our initial tendency to think saving the child is morally more incumbent on us in the former situation than in the latter. But Kamm believes the factor of distance (or proximity) makes a relevant moral difference in/between these two cases, and, in order to rule out other factors that might be thought to be determining our moral judgments in those cases (like whether others are in a position to help), she devises other examples that she believes bring out the intuitive and real moral force of the factor of distance (proximity).

Both Unger's book and Kamm's paper are very rich and extremely complicated, and what I have to say here won't go into every nook and cranny of what they say. But I find it interesting and a bit surprising that neither of them considers the moral importance of our empathic tendencies or capacities. For example, in denying the intuitive or actual moral relevance of distance, Unger comes up with a category of salience/conspicuousness (also with a category of the dramatic or exciting, but I will discuss that a bit later) that he does take to be relevant to our intuitive judgments, but never once considers how what one might easily take to be a related notion – what we can readily or immediately empathize with – might be relevant, or thought to be relevant, here. Similarly, Kamm considers and rejects what Unger says about salience or conspicuousness (she also talks about vividness) in favor of the idea that (complexly under-stood) spatial distance is relevant to distinguishing between cases like the drowning child and starving examples mentioned earlier, but somehow the subject of empathy never comes up.[4]

However, I believe the notion of empathy can help us sort out our intuitive reactions to the kinds of cases Singer, Unger, and Kamm describe better than the explanatory factors they mention, and let me say something about this now. In drowning examples, someone's danger or plight has a salience, con-spicuousness, vividness, and *immediacy* (a term that, for reasons mentioned below, I prefer, but that Singer, Unger, and Kamm don't use) that engages normal human empathy (and consequently arouses sympathy and caring con-cern) in a way that similar dangers we merely know *about* – dangers, we might say, that we know only *by description* – do not. The recent literature of devel-opmental psychology bears out this claim (and essentially the same point is made in Hume's *Treatise*).[5] So if morality centrally involves empathy-based concern for people, we are in a position not only to explain why a failure to help in the drowning case seems worse to us than a failure to give to famine relief, but also to justify that ordinary moral intuition – thereby undercutting Singer's arguments.

Given such an empathy-based approach, let's next consider what Kamm and Unger say about various cases. For example, in discussing the salience/con-spicuousness that Unger invokes in explaining our (for him misguided) intui-tions, Kamm distinguishes subjective and objective salience. Then, focusing on the former, she speaks of the science-fiction case of someone who can see a person suffering overseas with long-distance vision.[6] The suffering would then be salient, conspicuous, or vivid for the individual with the long-distance vision, but Kamm says that it is (intuitively) acceptable for that individual to 'turn off' her long distance vision (and pay no more attention to the fate of the person she has seen than to the fate of distant others she *hasn't* seen). But if she can turn it off, presumably she is also permitted simply to *turn away, avert her gaze*; and that is certainly implied by the view Kamm defends about the relevance of proximity.

However, I don't think this conclusion is in fact morally intuitive, and I believe considerations of empathy help to explain why. Turning away from someone we see (even if only at an extreme distance) seems *worse* than ignor-ing someone whom one knows about only by description; and assuming, for example, that one has the means instantly to deliver help either to someone whose danger or need one sees through long-distance vision, or to someone whose danger or need one merely knows about, most of us, I think, would consider it inhumane to turn away from the person whose plight one saw and then (coldly) decide to give the aid to someone one merely knew about. What is inhumane here arguably has something to do with empathy, with a failure of empathic response to someone whose need one perceives. The immediacy or vividness of such perceived need engages our (normal or fully developed)

23

human empathy more deeply or forcefully than need known only by description, and so a morality that highlights empathy in the way(s) I have been suggesting can account for and/or justify our moral reactions to Kamm's case here better than Kamm's appeal to (complexly contoured) spatial distance and proximity does; and it is difficult to see how Kamm can use this example to argue successfully against the view that subjective salience or vividness is relevant to our moral intuitions.

Interestingly, Kamm does say that what we see at an overseas distance would exert 'psychological pressure' on us to help. But she dismisses that pressure as somehow outside the bounds of our moral intuitions, because she thinks that we lack any intuition that tells us we have more obligation to the person we see than to someone we don't. If, however, and as I have just claimed, we do have such an intuition, then what she terms mere psychological pressure is in fact a moral intuition that her emphasis on distance fails to account for, but that a view that brings in empathy can.

Kamm then turns to an example of objective salience à la Unger. She imagines that the person with long-distance vision sees a group of people in trouble, and that one of the people is wearing a clown-suit and is much more dramatically exhibiting his need for help than the others. Kamm holds that this should make no moral difference to whom one feels one should help, and she uses this example to argue for distance as opposed to objective salience. But a view emphasizing empathy can also (and perhaps more fully) account for our intuitions about this kind of case. The person in danger of drowning or starvation who is in a clown-suit and busy waving his arms or making histrionic gestures may be more visibly obtrusive; but such a person may seem to be faking fear or pain, whereas someone else who is quieter or less demonstrative may bear the marks of suffering or anxiety more genuinely than the person in the clown-suit, and for that very reason more strongly engage our empathy. Such a case creates problems for an Ungerian objective-salience account of our moral intuitions, but not for a moral theory that appeals to empathy. Let us, however, consider a further example.

Unger denies that there is any intuitive or real moral difference between cases where an accident victim one can help is nearby and visible to one, and cases where the victim is at some distance and one learns about his plight via Morse code.[7] But Kamm thinks he is mistaken here about our intuitions, and claims the difference is due to the factor of distance;[8] and while I agree with Kamm that there is a significant difference between such cases, it seems to me, once again, more plausible – or perhaps I should say more promising – to explain it in terms of empathy.[9]

Kamm also says that even if proximity affects our duty to aid, it doesn't affect our duty not to harm: we have at least as strong a duty not to harm someone who is far as not to harm someone who is near. However, I believe this obscures some rather significant moral intuitions. Negative and positive duties may respond very differently to (sheer) proximity and distance, but I

24

believe they are affected somewhat similarly by considerations having to do with empathy.

Those who gunned down children and other civilians at My Lai saw their victims and killed them in cold blood, and I think we are more chilled, more horrified, by what they did than we are by the actions of those who killed children and other civilians from the air and never saw their victims. We also tend to believe that there is something morally worse about killing innocents in cold blood than about killing them (without actually seeing them) from a plane. And the difference here may well have to do with normally responsive human empathy. The person who is willing to kill innocents in cold blood acts more unfeelingly, demonstrates a greater lack of (normal or fully developed) empathy, than the person who kills from the air, and I therefore believe that considerations of empathy are relevant to the strength of our obligations not to kill and not just of our obligations to help, a point Kamm misses through her exclusive emphasis on (complexly contoured considerations of) distance.

Now, of course, we do think there is something cowardly and arrogant about killing from a safe distance, but this cowardice and this arrogance may characterize the military practice of aerial bombardment rather than individual airmen, who may have had little choice about how they would attack the enemy. What Lieutenant Calley did at My Lai he did on his own, whereas the individual airman who bombed civilians from a safe distance did so as part of a practice mandated and encouraged by military superiors, a practice that made it all too easy to kill civilians, and that one could regard as reflecting smug, arrogant, or cowardly attitudes on the part of a country possessing a total technical superiority over its enemy. If, therefore, we think of the aerial bombardments as being as bad as, or worse than, what was done at My Lai, that may be because the moral blameworthiness is so widespread, rather than because we really think what any individual airman/bombardier did was as morally bad as what Calley did acting on his own.[10]

At this point, we have illustrated the criterial moral relevance of (considerations of) natural human empathy using the example of our moral relations with the fetus, and we have gone on to discuss the importance of empathy for understanding cases, familiar from the literature that has grown up around Peter Singer's work, that involve issues about our obligations to people who we see or don't see, or who are near or far from us. The latter kinds of example all involve dangers or emergencies of one kind or another, but we have yet to consider another sort of danger/emergency that has sometimes been discussed by philosophers, cases where the issue is not so much (or cannot so easily be imagined to be) spatial proximity or distance, but rather *temporal* proximity or distance.

I am thinking of the well known example of miners trapped in a coal mine (as a result, say, of a cave-in). We typically feel morally impelled to help the miners rather than (at that point) expend an equivalent amount to install safety devices in the mines that will save a greater number of lives in the long run. But some have disagreed. Charles Fried discusses this example in his *An Anatomy of Values*, and claims that we/society should prefer to install the safety devices and let the miners die. (He gives his argument a rather barbaric flavor by saying we should even be willing to convey this decision to the ill-fated miners face-to-face, if that is somehow possible.)[11]

This example, this choice, doesn't turn on a contrast between near and far, or between what is perceived and what is not, because we can easily imagine that those who have to choose who to save are at a distance from the mine, and don't know or perceive either the trapped miners or those who might be in danger there in the future. We can well imagine, for example, that *we* somehow are empowered to make the choice, having heard or read reports of the mine cave-in, and I don't think the tendency to prefer saving the presently trapped miners would then be explainable in terms of an empathy-derived preference for saving those whose dangers we are perceptually aware of rather than those whose dangers we merely know about.

Still, if we have to choose between the presently trapped miners and those who may be in danger in the future, there is an immediacy to the danger the former are in that does, I think, engage our empathic/sympathetic juices in a way that the danger to the latter does not. Of course, there is also an immediacy to our previous example of a drowning child whose distress is (immediately) visible to us, but this immediacy, clearly, is perceptual and hinges on issues about the *spatial* distance that direct perception can accommodate. A rather different kind of immediacy is at issue in the miners example, an immediacy having more to do with the present-tense character of the miners' danger – the fact that it is a 'clear and present danger' – than with any spatial or spatially correlated factors. But both kinds of immediacy appeal to our empathy more forcefully than situations not involving these forms of immediacy tend to do. (The fact that the word 'present' applies both to a time and to a mode of sensory contact seems very apt, given this common appeal to empathy.)

Thus we may not see, or hear, or personally know the miners who are now trapped and, because they are thus known to us only as a class or by description, the empathic appeal of their plight – as compared with the plight of those who might be in danger later – is different from the empathic moral appeal of (dangers to) those we are perceptually aware of.[12] But it is natural to think of both kinds of case as involving some sort of immediacy, and that may be the best term for describing the (assumed?) objective correlate, in certain kinds of situation, of our (subjective or psychological) tendency toward empathy. And since we can use such correlated immediacy and empathy to explain our moral reactions both in the miners case and in the cases discussed in the Singer literature, we are given further reason to believe in the importance of empathy as a criterion for moral judgment.[13]

The notion of compassion also helps us here. Someone who prefers to invest in mine-safety equipment (and who is willing to convey that preference directly to the miners themselves) cannot be said to be compassionate, even if he or she seeks to save more lives.[14] And that is because compassion intersects with empathy and with immediacy in a fashion illustrated by the miners example. (Such intersection can also take place in various Singer-type proximity/perceivability cases.) It is because the person who decides to install safety devices shows a certain deficiency in empathy that we think of him or her as less compassionate and as acting less well than someone who would choose to save the presently trapped miners.[15] (More generally, though there is no time to show it here, we could say that compassion is empathy-based caring involved in a certain class of situations.)

Unger (*op. cit.*, pp. 78f.) describes a case in which a meteor has fallen to earth and will explode with disastrous results in a densely populated area unless someone immediately steals an 'Ejector' machine from its rightful owner and uses it to hurl the meteor to a deserted canyon. He thinks one is permitted to steal and operate the Ejector in such circumstances, but says that the 'dramaticness' of the trouble involved here makes no difference to that permission. Yet this example involves just the sort of clear and present danger that we saw in the case of the trapped miners, and if empathy is relevant to morality, then dramaticness (or at least what makes for drama in the case Unger describes, namely the clear and present danger) not only may make a difference to our intuitions, but may be criterially relevant to (the strength of) our actual moral obligations.

2. The Limits of Empathy and Obligation

I have said that both perceptual and temporal immediacy make one empathize more strongly with someone's plight (or, for that matter, opportunities) and (*pace* Singer, Unger, and Fried) are criterially relevant to the strength of our obligation(s) to aid. When someone's problem is out of sight (or more generally not perceived), or lies in the future, it seems, in a sense or metaphorically, more distant from us than a problem that we perceive and/or that affects us right now. But I think we now need to consider a further kind of empathy-affecting (and not literally spatial) distance we have not yet really focused on, one that any attempt to consider (the limits of) our obligations to distant or personally unknown groups of other people needs to take into account. This additional sort of distance can be characterized by its contrast with or opposition to the closeness or nearness that someone has (in differing degrees) to members of her own family. The phrase 'near and dear' standardly takes in both friends/partners/spouses and also members of one's family, but (for simplicity's sake, leaving aside family relationships that exist by marriage or adoption) family membership can be, and in essence therefore is, quite different from what is involved in friendship/partnership/marriage. Even very closely related members of the same family may not share their lives and their understanding of things in the way that friends and spouses typically do, and the feeling of familial closeness doesn't seem to depend on such forms of sharing. Rather, the kind of closeness involved here (and the distance that contrasts with it) is largely a matter of common (or an absence of common) *roots*.

The recognition of family connection, of common roots, gives rise in us to feelings of solidarity and affection, and seems to do so to a large extent independently of how much one shares of the life of (how far one feels spiritually at one with) someone connected by blood. If you think of yourself, for example, as a Patterson or a Sorvino, you feel a certain closeness or (this is not *just* a pun) kinship with other Pattersons or Sorvinos (unless they are not connected by blood and merely share a common name with you). Such family connection both provides an important part of most people's sense of identity and makes a difference to how easily we *identify with* certain people, and we find all these tendencies in a somewhat heightened form in the relations between parents and children. Parents feel tied to their children in a way that they *don't* feel tied to strangers, or even to those friends with whom they have the most in common and share the most; and by the same token children may feel a tie or feel close to their parents *independently* of how much they feel they can understand or share with (or be understood by) their parents. All this means that it is easier to identify and empathize with one's children and/or parents than with strangers, and our greater eagerness or willingness to help family members and the stronger obligations we have to family members can, I think, be understood in such terms (though I think there is no reason at this point to discuss further the various *degrees* of closeness that can exist within a family, and consequent differences in how obligated we may be to different family members).[16]

Now clearly friends and spouses typically share values, activities, and a history together in a way that makes mutual empathy easier and deeper than it is between strangers. So we are, at this point, aware of three different ways in which empathy can be strengthened: through perceptual and/or temporal immediacy, through family connection, and through the kinds of sharing that occur between friends and life-partners.[17] In all these cases, moral obligations to help seem intuitively stronger than when such factors are absent, and this constitutes strong support, I think, for the idea that empathy and differences of empathy can plausibly function as criteria for moral evaluation and moral distinction-making. But, then, what about all those cases where the above-mentioned factors are absent, all the people who we aren't friends with, who aren't part of our family, and who we never see?[18] We have moral obligations to such people, and any moral theory that denied this would seem totally unacceptable to most of us. But if moral obligation – and, in particular, the moral obligation to help people in need – is to be grounded in empathy, and empathy makes us favor friends, family, and the visible, will there be any empathy (left) for the vast majority of human beings (even leaving aside animals) who fall into none of these categories? And if that is a problem, how can empathy be used to account for what many of us think we owe by way of sympathy and help to such people?

But consider! Some people feel humanitarian concern for other people, for groups or causes they know about only indirectly or by description, and in discussing Hoffman's theory of the development of empathy, we mentioned his view that by the time they reach adolescence children have learned to empathize with groups or categories or classes of people who either are suffering or are disadvantaged in one way or another. Why shouldn't *this* kind of empathy – even if it lacks, so to speak, the props of immediacy, shared living, or family connection – be capable of giving psychological support to various sorts of activity on behalf of personally unknown or distant others?

If empathy of this sort exists, then we may be able to explain why we have obligations to (groups of) people we don't know, and at the same time also explain, in terms of the empathy-enhancing factors we have been talking about, why we owe *more* help to those who we see, or are friends with, or are related to, than to people who fall into none of these categories. Of course, Hume, in particular, expresses skepticism about our having obligations beyond the borders of our own country. He questions the very existence of such a thing as the love of humanity (as such) and also says that a person's generosity seldom extends beyond his native country.[19]

But I wonder whether Hume's opinion doesn't reflect certain limitations of his own time and circumstances, more than any inherent limit on the human capacity for empathy. In Hume's era, communication with distant parts of the world and the ability to affect distant parts of the world were far more limited than what is possible today. A large portion of humanity now lives in one (internationalized) world, something approaching a 'global village', if you will, and these changed circumstances may make it more realistic to envision people having genuine empathic concern for distant groups and nations than it perhaps was in Hume's day.

In addition, what Martin Hoffman calls 'inductive discipline' not only can help us to explain how empathy with distant groups can and does develop (by the time a child reaches adolescence), but also can indicate ways in which such empathy can be (further) increased or strengthened. As I mentioned earlier, induction in its earliest stages involves getting a child to recognize the harm he has caused *people he knows* (like a younger sibling or schoolmate) and teaching him both to put himself in their place and to be concerned about the harm his actions might cause them. But Hoffman also indicates how inductive techniques can be, and often are, extended so as to bring about or enhance an older child's concern for (groups of) people in other countries.

Both parents and schools can expose children to literature, films, or television programs that make the troubles and tragedies of distant or otherwise-unknown (groups of) people vivid to them; and they can encourage their sensitivity to such people by asking children to imagine – and getting them into the habit of imagining – how they or some family member(s) would feel if such things were happening to them. In addition, families, schools, and countries could provide for more international student exchanges than now exist, with visiting students living with local families and attending local schools – thus bringing home to both visitors and those visited the reality and real humanity of those who might otherwise just be names or descriptions. (I have read somewhere that such a program of exchanges between Palestinian and Israeli students is now under way in the Middle East.) Finally, parents and schools could inculcate in children the habit of thinking about, and being concerned about, the effects of their own actions and inactions (and those of their family, neighbors, and government) on the lives of people in other countries.[20]

Of course, the complete implementation of (all) these forms of moral education would require substantial resources and great commitment. But what we have said does give us a way of understanding how a full development of the natural human capacity for empathic concern for others might well include strong empathic concern for groups of people one didn't individually know, and even for humanity as a whole.

Interestingly, though, Martin Hoffman himself is somewhat skeptical about this possibility. At the very end of his recent book, he indicates some doubts about whether empathy can provide the basis for an adequate overall secular morality, and one of his main reasons seems to be that it is 'not natural' to apply his inductive techniques in the broad fashion that would be necessary in order for students to become (more) empathically concerned with (groups of) people in other parts of the world.[21]

But what is unnatural, or not natural, about the use of such techniques? Is it the fact that we/society probably wouldn't (in present circumstances) be willing to devote the necessary resources and energies to implementing them in large-scale fashion? But if that is the criterion of unnaturalness, then even inductive techniques that make a child more sensitive to the needs of those she is familiar with are unnatural. For predominant reliance on such techniques tends to be confined to middle-class parents, and many or most parents in a lower socio-economic position tend to use threats and what Hoffman and others call 'power assertion', rather than induction, to get their children to do what they want. And it is difficult to envisage any realistic way to mobilize present social and material forces so as to eliminate or sharply curtail the non-inductive forms of parental discipline. But I don't think Hoffman would want to call induction unnatural (or not natural) on this basis, so I don't think he has offered us a (consistent) reason for thinking it wouldn't be natural to sensitize school children more broadly to human problems through the extended or expanded inductive techniques described (so very briefly) just above.

In any event, realistic present expectations are hardly a definitive mark of what is within normal human capacities, and Hoffman's own rich and painstaking descriptions of the ways inductive techniques can be made to engage and realize our capacity for empathy make it seem to me quite plausible (or at least not implausible) to suppose that fully developed human empathy – the kind of empathy that would exist in human circumstances favorable to the overall development of empathy – can include a tendency toward and habit of active empathic concern for people one doesn't know. And it certainly leads me also to hope that unfolding human history will, in due course, bring about a greater and more widespread tendency/habit of this sort than what we find among human beings, most human beings, at present.

At this point, then, our accumulating examples and discussion make it possible, I think, to offer a general criterion of right and wrong action based in the notion of empathic caring or concern for others. Rather than say (as I said, roughly, in Chapter 1) that actions are wrong if, and only if, they reflect or exhibit or express a deficiency of caring motivation, one can claim that actions are morally wrong and contrary to moral obligation if, and only if, they reflect or exhibit or express an absence (or lack) of fully developed empathic concern for (or caring about) others on the part of the agent. (The 'others' could, in principle, include fetuses, animals, or what-have-you, and we shall take up the issue of supererogation, and of morally *admirable* or *good* action, in just a moment.)[22]

I believe all the kinds of example we have discussed here can be accommodated by, and therefore lend support to, the moral criterion just stated. We have spoken about concern for near and dear, and also about concern for distant and unknown others, and what the above criterion tells us, very roughly, is that acts that demonstrate empathic concern for near and dear may nonetheless count as wrong if at the same time they show a lack of normally or fully developed empathic concern for people we don't know. (Refusing to save a drowning child one has never seen before in order not to disappoint one's daughter by being absent when she returns home from school might be a good example of this.) And the criterion also tells us that there are cases where an act of helping strangers can be seen as morally wrong because it shows a lack of fully developed empathic concern, say, for one's own spouse, parents, or children.

However, the new criterion might seem problematic because the earlier point, that most of us haven't developed the fullest kind of human empathy, may lead one to wonder whether an ethics with moral standards based, in the manner just stated, on such an ideal doesn't violate the principle that 'ought' implies 'can'. If fully developed empathy is the touchstone of our *present* moral obligations, doesn't that mean that the many of us who are (at present or foreseeably) incapable of such empathy (we haven't, for example, been inductively trained or taught in the 'internationalist' way Hoffman describes) are unable to comply with our moral obligations to people in other countries?

I don't think so. For consider, to begin with, how similarly one might also attack those, like Peter Singer, Peter Unger, and Shelly Kagan, who espouse moral principles that are far more demanding than the principles most of us believe in, principles that lead to a moral requirement (very roughly) that we give away most (really *most*) of what we now possess in order to help those (most of whom are quite distant from us) whose situation is much less fortunate than our own.[23] Most of us start off rejecting such demanding principles, or at least being unwilling to conform to them, but it would surely be

31

unreasonable to reject those principles on the ground that our rejection/ unwillingness makes us *unable* to conform to them. The principles' defenders can claim, rather, that we are able, have it in our power, to do what they recommend, even if we reject the principles or are, for emotional or self-interested reasons, unwilling to follow them. 'Ought' implies 'can' is thus not violated, because all of us *could* give most of our money away to relieve suffering or prevent disasters in distant parts of the world (or, indeed, closer to home), and that is precisely what the more demanding moral principles consider to be obligatory for us. Moreover, Singer, Unger, and Kagan all believe, and make efforts to show, that proper moral consideration and moral education could move us to accept their moral principles, and so the (varying) approaches they take all arguably conform to 'ought' implies 'can' in what we might call the narrow sense and (perhaps even) to the reasonable condition that moral principles be consonant with general human capacities – what we might call the broad sense of 'ought' implies 'can'.

But there is no less (and perhaps considerably more) reason to believe that a morality based in fully developed human empathy conforms to these two versions of 'ought' implies 'can'. The narrow sense requires only that any given (adult, sane) moral agent be capable of avoiding wrongdoing (capable of doing what is obligatory), but, as I suggested earlier on, an ethic of caring, or of empathic caring, doesn't say that a person who doesn't care about others always acts wrongly or contrary to her obligations. It says, rather, that one acts wrongly if an act one performs reflects or exhibits the fact of one's uncaringness or, as I would now want to say, if it reflects or exhibits a lack of fully developed empathic caringness.

So, then, consider someone, s, who has relatively little empathic concern for human suffering (in the less-developed world). If we assume that fully developed empathic concern for others would lead most people to make some sort of contributions toward relieving such suffering, then s will exhibit a lack of such concern if s refuses to make any such contributions, and such refusal will count as wrong and contrary to s's obligations, according to the theory I am defending. But, of course, even with s's lack of empathy and concern, it still is within s's power to make a substantial contribution (even if we can be nearly certain that s won't do so). In that case, it is within s's power to fulfill the obligation to make a substantial charitable contribution, and, further, if s *were* to do so, such action or behavior wouldn't *reflect or exhibit* (what is in fact) s's deficiency of empathic concern or caring, and as a result would not count as wrong or contrary to moral obligation according to the ethics of care I am defending.[24] I therefore see no violation here of (the narrower sense of) 'ought' implies 'can'.

Of course, if everyone were quite literally under a moral obligation to have a substantial degree of empathic concern for other people, to have certain sentiments rather than others, then at any given time it *would* be impossible for empathically deficient individuals to fulfill their moral obligations, because one presumably cannot change one's emotional make-up or character at will. But

32

the theory I am defending doesn't assert any obligations to feel in certain ways. It may say that those who lack certain feelings are morally deficient or bad people (have morally deficient or bad character), but the only moral *obligations* it imposes are on human action. As I indicated just above, it doesn't claim that anyone has an obligation to have or act from caring motives; it only requires us *not* to act from uncaring motives, *not* to act in ways that reflect a lack of empathic concern for others.[25] And because, for the reasons mentioned, even the unempathic and the uncaring may be in a position to do *at least this much*, there is no violation of 'ought' implies 'can' in the narrower sense.[26]

From the perspective of the broader sense, too, there seems to be no *more* reason to think that empathy for distant groups of people is beyond our developed moral capacities than to think that conformity to the principles Singer *et al.* recommend is unsuited to our powers. In fact, rather, the various forms of partiality built into human empathy would naturally lead someone with fully developed empathic concern for others to resist making some of the choices that Singer *et al.* require in the name of overall or impartially considered good. So an ethic based in empathic caring gives us reason to believe that Singer-type principles are not morally binding on us because they require people to go beyond (and in a different, impartial direction from) the specific human capacities or powers that, according to the present theory, are most relevant to questions about our obligations to others.[27]

Now nothing I have said above indicates very precisely how strong our obligations to aid (distant) others actually are. But there is a reason – and I think a good reason – for this. If we (as individuals, as societies, as a species) haven't in fact yet made our best efforts to stimulate and educate our empathic capacities for concern with people we don't know, then we presumably don't know how far those capacities can or eventually will take us; and although I suspect (and have tentatively said) that those developed capacities wouldn't lead us to sacrifice our own welfare (and that of our family and friends) on behalf of distant others *to anything like the extent* that Singer, Unger, Kagan *et al.* regard as obligatory, I also believe that (more) fully developed empathic concern for others would lead to *greater personal sacrifices* than most of us now make and than are (or seem to be) required by Bernard Williams's well known views about the integrity of individual agents.[28]

So we have moral obligations to help strangers and people we only know about, but I propose at this point to remain somewhat vague about just how strong those obligations are. At the very least, though, I am and have been assuming that we are not obligated to give most of what we have away to those poorer than ourselves, and that our obligations to people we merely know about are less strong than those we have to friends and family and to people we actually see. But what about the rare individual who is willing to give much of what s/he has to the world's poor (while also meeting her obligations to help friends, family, etc.)? Wouldn't we find such a person morally admirable?

We would, indeed. Normal human self-interest or self-concern makes most people reluctant and, indeed, unwilling to give a great deal of their money away, and if someone, say, out of incredibly strong feeling of empathic concern for suffering but distant human beings gave up all luxury and even comfort in order to help them, we would intuitively regard such a person as having acted supererogatorily, as having in a most praiseworthy way gone beyond the call of duty.[29] But the fact of supererogation here can be accounted for or justified in the same terms we have been using in regard to other moral claims and distinctions.

To begin with, someone who gives less than such a person is not necessarily acting wrongly or demonstrating a lack of fully developed normal human empathy. After all, a human capacity can, in the ordinary sense, be fully developed in someone, but still allow for the possibility that others might display that capacity to an even greater extent, display it in a way that goes beyond all usual expectations and that shows a special talent or gift. Thus I am fully capable of driving a car; but others, such as chauffeurs and stunt drivers, may demonstrate more talent for driving than I do. I think I also have a fully developed normal human capacity for scheduling and planning things, yet there are other people who display an ability to plan or schedule far more remarkable than anything I or most other normal people are capable of. (Here and elsewhere I am treating normality as a statistical notion.) And something similar can happen in the moral realm.

Even if empathy is fully developed in certain people, (a very few) others might demonstrate an unusual and unexpected gift for empathy and for transcending or limiting their self-concern, and such individuals might give away more of their money than we would expect from anyone whose empathic concern for others had (merely) been fully developed.[30] But, then, this would be more money than it is necessary to give away in order to fulfill one's moral duty, according to the present view. So the person who demonstrates an unusually high degree of empathic concern for others – the person who demonstrates *more* empathy than most people with fully developed empathy ever show – can be said to act in a supererogatory fashion, and it is the criterial emphasis on empathy that allows care ethics to justify this claim.

Furthermore, the ability to accommodate moral supererogation in this way constitutes a real advantage over other approaches to ethics. Kantianism, utilitarianism, and both ancient and contemporary Aristotelian ethics are all uncomfortable with supererogation and are typically committed to assumptions that rule out the possibility of someone acting beyond the call of duty. To that extent, these views do much less justice to our moral intuitions than the ethics of empathic caring developed here.

However, at this point a very serious objection to using empathy as a moral criterion needs to be considered. We have seen how differences in empathy correlate with a large number of intuitive moral differences. But one may well wonder whether every natural distinction in or of empathy corresponds to

34

distinctions with intuitive moral force, and perhaps the greatest of these worries concerns possible differences between the empathy we may feel for people of a different (or opposite) race, religion, or sex/gender, and the empathy we feel toward people of our own race, religion, or sex/gender. If, for example, people tend to feel, or inevitably feel, more empathy for people of the same race than for people of a different race, does that really give us any moral reason or permission to favor those of the same race? Isn't this just the kind of case where morality should oppose our 'natural biases', and doesn't that therefore argue against grounding morality in feeling (empathy)?

These are good questions, but it will help to answer them if we consider whether in fact there is any very strong natural disposition toward greater empathy for people of one's own race (we can talk about sex and religion a bit later). Hoffman says that there is 'surprisingly little evidence' for such bias, but he notes at least one study that seems to indicate its existence in children.[31] Lawrence Blum and others have argued, however, that lesser empathy toward someone with a different skin color (or hair color, for that matter) may depend on what parents or society have conveyed to children about the value of different skin colors or about the need to distance oneself from people of certain skin colors, rather than on any innate predisposition.[32]

In addition, even if there turned out to be such a predisposition in very young children, that predisposition might fade over time with the child's increasing cognitive maturity (assuming the absence of social prejudice and enmity), just as the early tendency simply to empathize with another person's occurrent feelings eventually gives way, in the light of greater knowledge of the factors that affect human wellbeing, to empathic dispositions that take account of aspects of another person's situation that *transcend* the person's immediately occurrent feelings. (A child may feel pleasure at the pleasure of an adult who is obviously enjoying a certain activity, whereas, to use an example I mentioned earlier, an adult who knew that the first adult had terminal cancer might well have a less positive and even a negative empathic reaction to such temporary enjoyment in the light of her knowledge of what the person was soon going to be suffering.) At present, therefore, I think we have little reason to believe that people have an innate and long-term tendency, independent of social or family values, toward greater empathy with people of the same race or skin color, and so I don't think a moral philosophy that appeals to empathy is in any grave danger of justifying unjustifiable distinctions.[33]

And I would want to say similar things about the issue of sex or gender bias. Hoffman mentions a study that indicates that young children have a tendency to empathize more with those of the same sex, but also notes the tendency of (young) men to respond more empathically, or at least helpfully, to women in distress.[34] And, in addition, there is the well known tendency for defense attorneys to object to women jurors in cases when a woman, rather than a man, is on trial for a serious crime. I don't think we can know at this point whether social prejudices or stereotypes are responsible for (certain) mature adults' tendencies to be more sympathetic to the distress or danger of those of opposite sex, and at this point it is difficult to know whether there are any substantial and lasting innate tendencies toward more (or less) empathy for those of the same sex or gender. The ethics of empathy may here be hostage to future biological and psychological research, but I don't think that takes away from its *promise* as a way of understanding and justifying (a certain view of) morality. (There is also the somewhat different and extremely important question whether women are, on the whole, more empathic than men – but I prefer to take this up later on.)

However, the issue of religion, finally, seems somewhat different from sex/gender and race. People have more choice about their religion than about their sex/gender or race, and religious groups with a common history may possess or engender something closer to friendship than race or sex/gender by itself does. Compatriots in a republic can share in 'civic friendship', and such facts are often felt to be relevant to moral obligation. We are sometimes said to have stronger obligations to help compatriots than to help people in other countries, and an ethic based on empathy can certainly claim that, based on shared history and traditions, it may be easier to empathize with compatriots than with individuals in or from other countries. (More on this topic in Chapter 6.) Of course, such preference frequently degenerates into jingoism and (in the original sense) chauvinism, but there is no reason why an ethics of empathy has to treat this as morally acceptable. And similar points can be made about religion.

Though religion has too often divided people and led to something akin to, or worse than, jingoism (a topic to which we shall return in Chapter 4), those who share a religion typically share history and traditions in a way that increases mutual empathy. If there is such a thing as civic friendship, then perhaps we can also speak of 'credal friendship', and perhaps such friendship underlies and supports moral distinctions no less plausible than those that arise by virtue of common citizenship. Furthermore, given the actual history of the world, the members of certain races and the members of a certain gender/sex or religious groups may experience a solidarity born of common suffering or victimization. To take just one obvious example, blacks (or at least African-Americans) may find it easier to empathize with one another because of their common experience of discrimination and worse, and (for reasons that will become clearer in later chapters) an ethics of empathy need not treat these facts of history (rather than of innate disposition) as irrelevant to black people's, or others', moral obligations.[35]

Our ordinary thought about the morality of individual action divides, by and large, into two main categories: moral issues about beneficence or helping others, and moral issues about deontology. We have discussed our obligations to help others at some length in the present chapter, and we have done so within a sentimentalist care-ethical framework that appeals to empathy. Deontology, however, involves or imposes moral restrictions or limits on what one may permissibly do to help others (or oneself), and this makes it seem – strongly

36

seem – as if deontology stands in opposition to the caring motivation and psychological mechanisms of empathy that I have been speaking about. So finding a sentimentalist caring-ethical justification for deontology would appear to constitute a very large challenge, and I propose to take up that challenge in the next chapter.

Notes

1 Published originally as Peter Singer, 'Famine, Affluence, and Morality', *Philosophy and Public Affairs* 1, 1972, pp. 229–43.
2 Peter Unger, *Living High and Letting Die*, New York: Oxford University Press, 1996.
3 See Frances Kamm, 'Famine Ethics' in Dale Jamieson, ed., *Singer and His Critics*, Oxford: Blackwell, 1999, pp. 162–208.
4 I don't think Kamm ignores empathy because she thinks it too *subjective*. Unger's salience, as she notes, has a subjective aspect, but can also be viewed in a more objective way as what is, or would be, salient to a normal observer. But empathy also allows such a distinction, and the view I am defending focuses on what calls forth (more or less) empathy in a human being with a fully developed capacity for empathy.
5 For discussion of the greater empathy we tend to feel toward victims who are present to our senses, see Martin L. Hoffman: *Empathy and Moral Development: Implications for Caring and Justice*, Cambridge: Cambridge University Press, 2000, pp. 209ff.; Martin L. Hoffman, 'Empathy, its Limitations, and its Role in a Comprehensive Moral Theory' in W. Kurtines and J. Gewirtz, eds, *Morality, Moral Behavior, and Moral Development*, New York: John Wiley and Sons, 1984, p. 298; Martin L. Hoffman, 'Toward a Comprehensive Empathy-Based Theory of Prosocial Moral Development' in D. Stipek and A. Bohart, eds, *Constructive and Destructive Behavior*, Washington, DC: American Psychological Association, 2000/01, concluding section. For Hume's discussion of the same basic idea, see L. A. Selby-Bigge, ed., *A Treatise of Human Nature*, Oxford: Clarendon Press, 1958, p. 370 (also pp. 316ff.).
6 Frances Kamm, 'Famine Ethics', *op. cit.*, pp. 182f.
7 Peter Unger, *Living High and Letting Die*, *op. cit.*, esp. p. 36.
8 Frances Kamm, 'Famine Ethics', *op. cit.*, p. 184. Later in her article (p. 199) Kamm suggests some possible explanations of why distance matters, among them the hypothesis that it might be due to the fact that distance tracks potential cooperative relations. She argues, however, that this would not allow us to explain why distance seems to make a difference to our moral obligations to animals. But for reasons exactly similar to those mentioned earlier in connection with human examples, I think our obligations to animals depend more on perceptual factors connected with empathy than on sheer distance. It is morally worse to ignore the pain or plight of a dog one sees than of a dog one merely knows about, but that difference relates to natural human empathy rather than to distance or proximity as such.
9 Unger notes (*Living High and Letting Die*, *op. cit.*, p. 36) that such cases differ with respect to 'experiential impact', a notion that ties in with empathy. But he doesn't pay much attention to impact, presumably because he (mistakenly) thinks it makes no significant difference to our intuitions.
10 On the other hand, and as Marilyn Friedman has suggested to me, someone could simply claim that what Calley did was more morally blameworthy *but not morally worse* than what the individual airman did. However, I don't think we have any good reason to accept such a view.
11 See Charles Fried, *An Anatomy of Values: Problems of Personal and Social Choice*, Cambridge, MA: Harvard University Press, 1970, pp. 207–27, esp. p. 226. Incidentally,

as hypothetical examples don't evoke empathy and compassion the way actual situations do (for those who are in them), someone who forgets/ignores the significance of empathy may be led to make an overly impartial recommendation regarding what to do in some hypothetical situation. This may be part of the explanation of Fried's callous recommendation about what to do with the trapped miners. I am indebted here to Phyllis Rooney, 'A Different Different Voice: On the Feminist Challenge in Moral Theory', *Philosophical Forum* XXII, 1991, pp. 335–61, esp. p. 351. Also see Carol Gilligan, *In a Different Voice*, Cambridge, MA: Harvard University Press, 1982, pp. 100f.

12 I want to say that the empathic appeal of future dangers tends to be less than that of present dangers to people we don't perceive, and that the appeal of the latter, in turn, is less than the appeal of dangers (to people) we actually perceive. But these different levels of empathic appeal can and do all operate through what Hoffman calls mediated association. (See Martin L. Hoffman, *Empathy and Moral Development*, *op. cit.*, pp. 49ff.) Even if empathy for unperceived miners requires us to have sophisticated concepts and linguistic skills, the arousal of such empathy can occur involuntarily (via association), rather than requiring the deliberate mental act of putting oneself in the miners' shoes (projective empathy). But, of course, empathy regarding the kinds of cases we have been talking about can, and frequently does, also work through projective empathy.

13 Hoffman's discussion of the empathic 'bias' toward what is immediate includes both spatial/perceptual and temporal examples. See Martin L. Hoffman: 'Empathy, its Limitations, and its Role in a Comprehensive Moral Theory', *op. cit.*; *Empathy and Moral Development*, *op. cit.*, Ch. 8; and the final section of 'Toward a Comprehensive Empathy-Based Theory of Prosocial Moral Development', *op. cit.* Also, Bernard Williams, *Ethics and the Limits of Philosophy* (Cambridge, MA: Harvard, 1985, pp. 185f.) stresses the moral importance of immediacy, but gives a confusing account of that notion. (See Elizabeth Ashford, 'Utilitarianism, Integrity, and Partiality', *Journal of Philosophy* XCVII, 2000, pp. 421–29.) My view here is that the importance of immediacy is best defended by reference to empathy.

14 I am and have been assuming that the number of lives that can be saved by installing safety devices isn't totally out of proportion to the number of miners one can currently rescue. But if, say, ten times as many miners can be saved by the use of the new safety devices (and there is an 'either–or' choice), then the sheer magnitude of the difference can change our intuitions, feelings, and judgments about this kind of case. A willingness to allow currently endangered miners to die in order to be able to save ten times more miners in the future doesn't have to reflect (what we would call) a lack of compassion. For further consideration of how the magnitude of sheer numbers can affect our empathic reactions and moral judgments, see the discussion of deontology in the next chapter.

15 Of course, act-utilitarianism recommends that one install the safety devices rather than save the miners, and to the objection that this would show a deficiency of compassion, the utilitarian can always reply that *saving* the trapped miners would show a deficiency of universal benevolence. This would naturally leave many of us still feeling that there was something deplorably cold and calculating with not being compassionate in the miners' case, but I think a systematic reliance on the notion of empathy as a moral criterion helps to give *moral–theoretic weight* to that persisting reaction.

16 On the ways in which a sense of family connection creates and/or constitutes a greater identification and empathy with members of one's own family, see Elliott Sober and David Sloan Wilson, *Unto Others*, Cambridge, MA: Harvard University Press, 1998, p. 233.

17 Hume holds that family connection, friendship, and both temporal and perceptual immediacy all make for stronger operation of the mechanisms of sympathy/empathy and stronger consequent concern for certain others. See e.g. L. A. Selby-Bigge (ed.), *A Treatise of Human Nature, op. cit.*, esp. pp. 370, 386, 389.

18 Here, in order to keep things simpler, I shall deliberately ignore issues of temporal immediacy. If there are problems about eliciting empathic concern for contemporaries who we don't know (and who are not part of our family), there are even greater problems in connection with future generations (especially if many of us are going to leave no descendants). I think the notion of empathy can be used to clarify questions about our obligations to future generations – as far as I know no-one has tried to do this yet – but I want to leave discussion of this issue to another occasion. I am indebted to Larry Temkin for making me aware of the potential usefulness of the notion of empathy with regard to this problem.

19 See L. A. Selby-Bigge (ed.), *A Treatise of Human Nature, op. cit.*, pp. 481f., 602.

20 On these points, see Martin L. Hoffman, 'The Contribution of Empathy to Justice and Moral Judgment' in N. Eisenberg and J. Strayer, *Empathy and its Development*, New York: Cambridge University Press, 1990, esp. p. 69; Martin L. Hoffman, *Empathy and Moral Development, op. cit.*, p. 297.

Martha Nussbaum, 'Compassion: The Basic Social Emotion' (in Ellen Frankel Paul, Fred Miller Jr and Jeffrey Paul, eds, *The Communitarian Challenge to Liberalism*, Cambridge: Cambridge University Press, 1996, pp. 27–58) expresses a similar view about the importance for moral education of using literature, etc. to foster imaginative understanding of the sufferings of (otherwise unfamiliar) other people. Finally, I should mention that Virginia Held, 'The Ethics of Care' (in D. Copp. ed., *The Oxford Handbook of Ethical Theory*, Oxford: Oxford University Press, 2006, p. 550) points out that, from the standpoint of an ethics of care, both our concern for those we know *and* our concern for distant others should be characterized by responsiveness to needs and a willingness to understand things from someone else's point of view. This at the very least points in the direction of the more specific moral and moral–psychological claims I am making in the text above.

21 Martin L. Hoffman, *Empathy and Moral Development, op. cit.*, p. 298.

22 Someone who doesn't give (much) help to others on a given occasion when help is needed may not show herself to lack fully developed concern for others – if she has, for example, recently been doing a lot of other things for people. There can be such a thing as 'compassion fatigue' (see Martin L. Hoffman, *Empathy and Moral Development, op. cit.*, pp. 198ff.), and that notion helps our approach to make sense of the idea of imperfect duty. (I am indebted here to discussion with Kristin Borgwald.)

23 See especially Shelly Kagan, *The Limits of Morality*, Oxford: Clarendon Press, 1989.

24 This example raises some interesting questions about the individuation of actions that I think are best left to another occasion. I am indebted on this point to Scott Gelfand.

25 Michael Brady, 'Some Worries about Normative and Metaethical Sentimentalism', *Metaphilosophy* 34, 2003, pp. 145f. wonders whether my views don't have the implausible implication that a person who tries to become more empathically caring acts wrongly, because his or her efforts express or exhibit a deficiency of empathic caring. But if someone correctly *asserts* that he lacks full empathy, his assertion *describes* the lack of empathy but surely doesn't exhibit or express that lack; and by the same token an effort to become more empathic may *presuppose* or *assume* a lack of full empathy but doesn't seem to *express, exhibit*, or *display* that lack of empathy.

26 But don't parents have an obligation to love their children and act lovingly toward them? And doesn't this raise 'ought' implies 'can' problems for our theory? Perhaps it does. But one could also say that the most parents owe children is to act *as if they*

loved them. If (even) that is impossible for certain parents, we might prefer to say that they had an obligation not to have children in the first place, rather than say that they are violating present obligations when they do all kinds of things for their children but don't actually act as if they love them (assume the children can tell the difference!). I really don't know what to say about this issue. (I would like to thank Marilyn Friedman for calling it to my attention.)

27 On the other hand, Martin Hoffman seems to believe that morality requires more than (our fully developed powers of) empathy, because human empathy embodies a 'bias' in favor of near and dear that no amount of inductive or other training/education could ever eliminate, whereas morality has to be 'impartial'. (Martin L. Hoffman, *Empathy and Moral Development*, op. cit., pp. 216, 297f.; Martin L. Hoffman, 'The Contribution of Empathy to Justice and Moral Judgment', op. cit., pp. 76, 78n.) Here, however, I think Hoffman is somewhat misled by the fact that the philosophers and educationists he principally engages – Rawls and Kohlberg – insist that morality is or should be impartial. Although Hoffman refers to Lawrence Blum's *Friendship, Altruism, and Morality* (London: Routledge & Kegan Paul, 1980) as an example of recent moral partialism, the absence of other references to the partialist literature makes me wonder whether he is aware of how strong the current of partialism in present-day ethics really is.

A partialist (like myself) doesn't have to consider partiality toward one's family or toward those one sees as a bias in anything like a negative sense. Because it is very much open to the partialist to regard an *absence* of bias/partiality toward family, and even (as pointed out above) toward those one actually sees, as morally *less than ideal*, the partialist needn't share Hoffman's fears/reservations. However, Peter Singer in 'A Response [to Critics]' (in Dale Jamieson, ed., *Singer and His Critics*, Oxford: Blackwell, 1999, p. 308) says that partialists have failed to provide adequate foundations for their approach(es), and I take it that this is what a partialist ethic of empathic caring must attempt to do.

28 Bernard Williams, 'A Critique of Utilitarianism' in J. Smart and B. Williams, *Utilitarianism: for and against*, Cambridge: Cambridge University Press, 1973.

29 I am assuming here that the person with great empathy doesn't feel worthless and doesn't act on behalf of others because s/he doesn't feel s/he deserves anything good. Much selflessness and self-abnegation in favor of others may rest on feelings of unworthiness or a lack of self-respect, but it is not clear to me that such feelings/attitudes are psychologically compatible with great empathy for others. In any event, unusually strong empathy arguably doesn't have to rest on a sense of worthlessness, and I assume as much in the text. As we shall see in Chapter 4, a sense of worthlessness and selflessness can come from being treated in a non-empathic manner by parents or guardians, and the psychological literature indicates that children become empathic by being treated empathically. (See e.g. R. Koestner, C. Franz and J. Weinberger, 'The Family Origins of Empathic Concern: A 26-Year Longitudinal Study', *Journal of Personality and Social Psychology* 58, 1990, pp. 709–17.) This fits in well with what Hoffman and others have said about the superiority of inductive discipline over 'power assertion' as a way of creating/sustaining altruistic motivation. For a parent who tries to get his child to understand the distress of another already demonstrates empathy for that other, and there is nothing in power assertion that indicates empathy. In that case, further, the superiority of induction supports the familiar idea that children learn morality from parental or other *models*. (On this point see Nancy Eisenberg, *The Caring Child*, Cambridge, MA: Harvard University Press, 1992, Chs 7 and 8.)

30 There is a good deal of evidence that our capacity for empathy and altruism may, to a certain extent, depend on hereditary/temperamental factors. See e.g. Eisenberg, N.,

Guthrie, I. K., Murphy, B. C., Shepard, S. A., Cumberland, A. and Carlo, G., 'Consistency and Development of Prosocial Dispositions: A Longitudinal Study', *Child Development* 70, 1999, pp. 1360–72.

31 Martin L. Hoffman, *Empathy and Moral Development*, op. cit., p. 207.

32 On these points, see Lawrence Blum, 'Moral Development and Conceptions of Morality', in his *Moral Perception and Particularity*, New York: Cambridge University Press, 1994, p. 194; but also Mark A. Barnett, 'Empathy and Related Responses in Children' in Eisenberg and Strayer, *Empathy and its Development*, op. cit., pp. 154ff.; M. Radke-Yarow, C. Zahn-Waxler and M. Chapman, 'Children's Prosocial Dispositions and Behavior' in P. H. Mussen, ed., *Handbook of Child Psychology*, New York: Wiley, 1983, esp. p. 514; Nancy Eisenberg, *The Caring Child*, op. cit., p. 138 (and works in footnotes).

However, as Nancy Eisenberg has pointed out to me, there is some evidence that children (and people generally) don't understand the facial expressions of those culturally or racially dissimilar to themselves as well as they understand the expressions of those more similar or familiar. This fact, together with an evolution-based tendency to fear what is different or unfamiliar, may then represent a kind of excusing/justifying condition of lesser responsiveness to those who are different – at least before knowledge, in the absence of conditions of prejudice, obviates the fear of difference and the lesser ability to empathize. This might explain and support the differential reactions of children, while at the same time helping to ground and justify equal treatment (*vis-à-vis* those similar and those dissimilar to one) in adults.

33 Jorge Garcia, 'The Heart of Racism', *Journal of Social Philosophy* 27, 1996, pp. 5–45 argues that a preference for people of one's own race may not be morally objectionable – and may even be morally called for or desirable – if it doesn't involve hatred or indifference toward people of other races. This might be true, and if it is, then the possibility that human beings may turn out to have a deep-seated tendency to empathize somewhat more with people of their own race poses no threat to the present empathy-based approach to morality. Hatred or prejudice (in the usual sense) toward other races could show a morally criticizable deficiency of empathic development, even if mere preference for one's own race did not. Similar points *may* hold with regard to same-sex preferences as well, though the burden of argument in that case seems to me to be somewhat heavier than with same-race preferences. I shall offer a specific care-ethical account of what is wrong with prejudice and hatred toward other groups in Chapters 4–6.

34 Martin L. Hoffman, *Empathy and Moral Development*, op. cit., p. 208. See also Nancy Eisenberg, *The Caring Child*, op. cit., pp. 39f., 139 (and works in footnotes).

35 The shared history of whites will not be relevant in this way to the obligations of whites, for two basic reasons. First, to the extent that whites have oppressed blacks, there will be an empathic basis for trying to make amends for that oppression, and this certainly will have some force against whites' preferring whites. But second, and as we shall see later in Chapter 6, it is easier for us to empathize with painful or bad psychological states than with pleasant or enviable ones, and so the empathic solidarity shared among whites is unlikely to be as strong as what blacks share, and this means, again, that it is (other things being equal) better or more acceptable for blacks to prefer blacks than for whites to prefer whites. (Similar points could be made about solidarity among females as compared with solidarity among males.)

3

DEONTOLOGY

1. Empathy and Harming

We have seen how an ethics of empathic care can deal with issues of helping others, and it is time now to see whether and how it can handle deontology. I am going to assume that my readers know what deontology is, but let me just briefly remind you that the idea of deontological restrictions is typically regarded as involving the assumption that certain sorts of positive acts or commissions – such as killing, injuring, stealing, lying, and breaking promises – are inherently (at least *prima facie*) wrong. One way of conceiving this wrongness (that it makes sense to focus on here) is to think of the positive actions as morally worse than corresponding negative acts, or omissions, that have similar consequences: for example, killing the innocent as worse than letting innocent people die. And act-consequentialism and act-utilitarianism precisely refuse to make such a distinction, thus rejecting, at least at ground-floor level, the whole of deontology. In doing so, the utilitarian regards all of morality as involving issues of helping people (or sentient beings), and since this helping is supposed to be understood as impartial between or among all individuals, utilitarianism is naturally seen as treating all of morality as a matter of *beneficence*.

However, we have seen how the contours of an intuitively plausible partialistic morality can be understood and justified by reference to differences of empathy, and beneficence hardly seems the right word for what a person does for those near and dear to her. What we have so far been talking about, then, is a morality of empathic caring, where caring takes in not only the attitudes/ motives people have, or are supposed to have, toward intimates, but also less strongly felt but still substantial humanitarian concern for distant and/or personally unknown others. (This terminology doesn't distort ordinary usage of the term 'caring'.) We have therefore already argued against utilitarian/consequentialistic impartialism, and the question now before us is whether we should reject another aspect of utilitarianism, *its* rejection of deontology. I submit that we have two strong reasons for doing so.

First, deontology is very plausible, very compelling. It just seems wrong, to refer to a familiar but very hypothetical example, for a surgeon secretly to kill one innocent person in order to harvest that person's organs and thereby save, say, five accident victims. One reason why Kantians object so strenuously to act-utilitarianism is the fact that the latter denies our deepest deontological intuitions; of course, Kantians themselves seek to justify deontology by reference to one or another version of the Categorical Imperative. If we give up on deontology, then from a moral-theoretic standpoint that will count as a great loss in intuitive plausibility for care ethics.

Second, the ethics of caring is actually in a less good position to deny deontology than is act-consequentialism. The latter, which includes act-utilitarianism, allows agents to violate deontological restrictions on killing, stealing, and the like only when doing so is *in impartialist terms* for the best. And such a consideration is plausibly seen as offering *some* sort of reason for violating the restriction. But any partialist ethics takes it as permissible and good to favor one's own near and dear over other people: for example, to save a spouse from drowning rather than some stranger. But in that case, if deontology is denied, it is hard to see how a partialist ethics like the ethics of care can avoid allowing and perhaps even mandating the *killing* of a stranger in order to save one's own spouse. This seems morally much more suspect, much less plausible, than the idea that we may kill one person when doing so will be for the impartially considered best. So I think an ethics of care has even more reason than consequentialism to hold onto deontology. But how is it to do that?[1]

Care ethicists have made few efforts in the past to justify deontology, and they have certainly not sought to ground it in empathy.[2] But that is what I am going to propose here. We have seen that empathy helps give rise to various kinds of helping responses, but we shall now see that empathy can also cause us to *refuse* to help – or be *unwilling* to help – in certain kinds of ways and in certain kinds of circumstances. If helping involves an emotional sensitivity to the factors we have previously been speaking of, then the refusal to help that underlies deontology involves an emotional sensitivity of a slightly different sort that I am going to describe in what follows. And the ability to see deontology as arising from the sentimental, rather than the rational or intellectual, side of our nature is crucial to the present attempt to give a caring-ethical account of the whole of morality. Thus the initially plausible supposition that deontological restrictions necessarily involve the sentimental side of our nature being limited *by some factor external to it* is going to turn out to be mistaken. Let us see how.

In the previous chapter it was shown that empathy works through certain *modalities* or *aspects* of an agent's interaction with the world. Agents are more empathic and empathically concerned with what *they perceive* than with what they don't; and they are also empathically more sensitive to what *they know to be going on at the same time* as their decision making and choices. These differences of empathy correspond to what we naturally think of as the greater immediacy of dangers that we perceive or that are contemporaneous with our concern. But there are other facts about, or factors in, our interactions with the

43

world that empathy is also sensitive to, and that give rise to a form of immediacy we have not yet mentioned.

When we cause a death, kill someone, we are in causal terms more strongly connected to a death than if we merely allow someone to die, and I believe that we are empathically sensitive to this distinction in a way that allows us to make sense of certain central issues of or in deontology. Given the role of empathy as discussed earlier, the strength of one's obligations regarding another person's distress can vary with whether one perceives that distress, or whether the distress is contemporaneous. But if we are also empathically sensitive to the strength of our causal relations to various forms of distress or harm, then an ethics of empathic caring can say that it is morally worse to kill than to allow to die, and a major part of ordinary deontology can then be accounted for in sentimentalist terms. And I believe there are intuitive reasons for thinking that we are empathically sensitive to doing versus allowing in the way just suggested.

If we are empathically more sensitive to perceived or contemporaneous (potential) pain, so too do we seem to be empathically more sensitive to (potentially) causing pain (or death) than to (potentially) allowing it. We emotionally *flinch* from causing or inflicting pain in a way, or to an extent, that we don't flinch from (merely) allowing pain, and I want to say that pain or harm that we (may) cause has, therefore, a greater *causal* immediacy for us than pain or harm that we (may) merely allow. This immediacy is quite parallel or analogous to the greater perceptual and temporal immediacy of what is, respectively, perceived or contemporaneous.[3] In that case, and given the moral weight I have argued we should give to our empathic reactions, we have some reason to conclude that it is morally worse to kill or harm than, other things being equal, to allow these things to happen, and that helps in our efforts to give a sentimentalist caring-ethical justification for deontology.[4]

Now it is well known that the intuitions most people have about killing versus letting die are not absolutist. We may think it is wrong to kill one in order to save five, but we aren't nearly so sure when it comes to 20 or 30 people, and we have some tendency to think it is wrong *not* to kill some one innocent person, if that is the only way to save a huge number of innocent lives. One nice feature of the attempt to explain the deontology of killing and harming in terms of empathy is that it helps to account for the conditional or limited force of what we intuitively regard as our obligations not to kill or harm. Killing, for example, does put us as agents in a shockingly closer connection to someone's harm than does allowing someone to die. It typically evokes a much more negative empathic response, of the thing as something to be avoided, than allowing to die. But our empathic reactions can sometimes come into conflict, and this presumably would happen, for example, if we had a choice between killing two people and allowing a thousand (or more) to die. Our strong empathic aversion to causing deaths might in such a case be overwhelmed by our empathic reaction to the sheer size or enormity of the loss of life that will be sustained if one *doesn't* kill the two people. One might then prefer to kill the two. And something similar might happen in regard to trapped miners. If installing safety equipment would definitely save *ten times* more lives in the future – and there is no other money available – then our sensitivity to temporal immediacy might be swamped by our empathically influenced sense of the enormity of the gains to be obtained by installing the equipment.[5] We might then (with wrenching sadness) let the contemporaneously endangered miners die.

Such examples demonstrate how well facts about stronger and weaker empathy correlate with some of the fine (or not-so-fine) moral distinctions we find it plausible to make. And they also support the caring-ethical thought that deontology isn't a matter of principles or rules or rational considerations that oppose the sentiments, but rather arises from, or can be understood in terms of, the sentiments themselves. But more needs to be said about deontology at this point – so far we have been talking just of killing and (bodily) harming. Deontology also covers issues about property, fidelity to promises, and truthtelling.

2. Property, Promises, and Truthfulness

I want to begin by discussing how considerations of empathy give us a way of understanding what is wrong with stealing other people's property. Most cases of theft occur against a background of conventions or laws governing property, but for present purposes I don't think we need to assume that this is necessarily the case. One set of cavemen might steal meat that another group had obtained through hunting – it doesn't seem absurd to speak this way, and in what follows I will assume that such behavior can really count as stealing.

Now when we take someone's property or possessions we typically harm them; in most cases, we directly cause them to be worse off than they were or otherwise would have been.[6] And this is different from merely allowing someone else to take a person's property or possessions. Thus the difference between causing harm and allowing harm applies to stealing as much as it does to the infliction of bodily harm, including killing, and the empathic appreciation of the distinction between causing and allowing harm can therefore serve as a criterion for deontological moral distinctions between actions and inactions regarding property. Empathic concern for (the welfare of) other people makes us not want to see them lose their possessions, but we are empathically more averse to causing such loss or harm than to allowing such losses or harms to occur through the agency of third parties or as a result of natural forces (that we are in a position to counteract). So empathy allows us to make a moral distinction between stealing property or possessions and merely allowing them to be taken (or stolen or destroyed), which we consider less bad. Let us next consider what our approach can say about promises and promise-keeping.

Many philosophers have sought to understand the morality of promising by reference to appropriate conventions or to just (enough) institutions. However, other philosophers – and not just utilitarians – have disagreed. Both Neil MacCormick and T. M. Scanlon treat our obligations in regard to promising as derived (very roughly) from obligations not to induce and disappoint certain sorts of expectation, and they hold further that we can violate the latter obligations even without having actually promised to do things.[7] What they both say comes very close to what a care-ethical account of promising in terms of empathy needs to say, but in what follows I focus more on Scanlon's fuller account of promising.

According to Scanlon, when we wrongfully break a promise or make a false promise, the wrongness involved is no different from that involved in disappointing expectations that haven't been induced by (making use of the conventions governing) promises. So even if the conventions or social practices governing the making of promises can make it easier both to create certain expectations and to commit the wrong of disappointing them (or of creating them in the first place), those conventions and practices 'play no essential role in explaining' the wrong involved here.[8] I think Scanlon – and MacCormick – are on the right track here, but I believe that our ethics of empathic care can make sense of these ideas in its own distinctive terms. I want to follow Scanlon and MacCormick in emphasizing the moral significance of inducing and disappointing expectations, but I think that significance is best brought out in terms of (developed) empathic concern for other people. When it is wrong to make a false promise or break a promise, that wrongness, I want to say, is justified by our empathic aversion to certain ways of creating and disappointing expectations. And none of the argument will need to appeal to conventions or to background, just institutions.

Let us begin, then, with a typical example of promise-breaking. A person induces someone to help him by promising to help the other in return, but then fails to help the other person, once the latter has performed his part of the bargain. This seems a very clear case of wrongdoing, but can it be accounted for in sentimentalist, care-ethical terms? Well, the person who breaks his promise has presumably led the promisee to expend some effort in the belief that the promiser will then expend a similar effort on his behalf. But if the promise isn't kept, then the promisee has expended that effort in vain, has borne a burden, even perhaps endured a certain amount of hardship, without having anything to show for it. To that extent, the promiser has had an influence for the worse on the promisee's life. He has induced him to act in a way that constitutes a net loss in his life. In order to simplify our discussion, I shall for now ignore other possible losses the promisee may have been induced to incur.

Contrast the situation of the promiser in our example with that of a bystander who sees that the promiser is not going to reciprocate. Imagine further that this bystander could help the promisee in the way the promiser promised to do, but decides not to do so (he may not need the promisee's help in return).This may not be wrong on the part of the bystander, and the difference between his inaction and the wrongness of actually breaking a promise can be understood by reference to some of the same empathic factors we have been using up till now in discussing the deontology of killing, harming, stealing, etc. Even if the bystander allows the promisee to suffer an uncompensated loss, he still doesn't induce the promisee to assume a burden in vain, and so his causal influence on the loss sustained by the promisee is far less than that of the promiser. But if the promiser and his actions thus have a causally more immediate relation to the harm or loss sustained by the promisee than anything done by the bystander, then we have a basis for saying that the promiser acts wrongly and the bystander does not. A normally empathic person will be more averse to standing in such a causally more immediate relation to a human loss or harm than to merely allowing a loss to occur, and the difference here is similar to the empathic difference discussed earlier between killing and allowing to die. By the same token, if we rework the above example so that the promiser has to choose between keeping his own promise and doing what some *other* promiser has promised but refused to do for someone else, he does wrong if he doesn't keep his own promise, and that too is understandable by reference to the fact that normal human empathy is *more* averse to actions that have *greater* causal impact on human loss, harm, or injury.

But the above cases differ from those involving the choice between doing and allowing bodily harm, and between killing and letting die, in two important respects. First, when someone sustains a loss because he has relied on another person's promise, it would be odd to say that the promiser caused the loss, at least in part because it would be odd to say that the promiser caused the promisee to rely on his word. Where someone's causal influence on an event goes through someone else's decision(-making), it is odd to say that they cause that event, so it is more natural to say that the promiser *influenced* or *induced* the promisee to rely on his word than that he caused him to. But even if this means that we can't or shouldn't say that he causes the loss sustained by the promisee, the words 'influence' and 'induce' both indicate a stronger causal impact on what happens to the promisee than a mere allowing would have.

The second point about causality arises from the fact that the promiser's causal influence on the loss or harm occurs in two temporal stages. He first induces the promisee to rely on his word and help him out, and then, after having been helped, he refuses to reciprocate. And one might wonder *when* the causal difference from cases involving the mere allowing of a loss actually occurs and whether, in particular, it may not be over by the time the person decides not to keep his promise – assuming it wasn't a false promise in the first place. After all, by the time he has to decide whether to reciprocate, the actions by means of which he induced the promisee to perform are in the past, and he need do nothing further in order for the promisee's expectations to be disappointed. So his failure to help in return may be conceived in just that way, as a failure or omission, rather than as having any more robust causal influence on the loss sustained by the promise. Why, then, should it count as any worse in moral terms than merely allowing *someone else's* promise not to be fulfilled?

But in order for someone to break a promise, he first has to make a promise, so in order for a promise to be broken, two different and presumably non-simultaneous events have to occur, and the two events together may exert a causal influence stronger than mere allowing on the loss that occurs to the promisee.[9] If promise-breaking involves a certain causality that we empathically shy from, that causality may be exerted over time rather than at a single time, so it would still be wrong, in deontological terms, to perform the joint and temporally extended act of making and breaking a promise. This has a number of implications.

It implies that a caring or empathic person will be reluctant to make a promise she doesn't think she can keep. It also implies that such a person will be reluctant to make a promise she has no intention of keeping (even though she could keep it). If one knows that one would never do something, even if one promised to do it, then to promise it is to make a lying promise and also to initiate a process that will involve one in having the same negative causal impact on someone that one has when one, in good faith, induces someone to rely on a promise but then disappoints their expectations. Because we empathically shy away from having such a causal influence for ill, we will be motivated in empathic terms not to make such a promise, and the wrongness of making a lying promise can therefore be understood in our caring-empathic terms.

Thus far, then, we have an empathic/causal explanation of why we shouldn't make a lying promise that induces someone to help us by making them expect that we will reciprocate, and also of why the total act of promising (perhaps in good faith) and breaking the promise is wrong. But this still leaves the wrongness of the later act of non-reciprocation, the later breaking of the promise, unaccounted for, and since such non-performance seems causally in the same boat as merely allowing harm or loss, there may at this point appear to be no way for a sentimentalist approach that appeals to empathic sensitivity to causal differences to account for the wrongness of the latter act. But that appearance is, I think, misleading.

Consider a situation where I administer poison to person x and have the antidote available. Imagine that another person has administered the same poison to person y. It is worse for me not to provide the antidote to x than to fail to provide it to y, and the distinction here is essentially deontological: if I fail to give the antidote to x, I can be said to have killed x, but I won't have killed y if I fail to provide y with the antidote, because I didn't poison y in the first place. But still a failure to provide x with the antidote seems to be just an omission – so how can deontology actually be in play here?

The answer may be that, in certain contexts, what would otherwise be an omission is actually a commission, or at least isn't purely an omission. After poison has been administered to both x and y, it presumably can't accurately be said that if I don't provide an antidote for x, I will (thereby) kill him. But it can be said that if I don't provide the antidote, I *will have* killed him. And if, as we have been assuming, one can flinch from the harm that one knows one *will do* if one performs an act, why can't one also empathically flinch from the harm that (one knows) one *will have done* to someone if one performs a certain act? Even if not providing an antidote is an inaction, it is also an essential part of a total action that is not yet completed, and it would be understandable if people could be empathically sensitive to and flinch from such total actions at any time when it is still possible to avoid their being (or having been) completed.

So one might be sensitive to the fact that if one fails to provide *x* with an antidote, one will have caused a harm, a death, to occur, and this may make one much more averse to this failure or omission than to the failure or omission involved in not providing *y* with an antidote. This motivational difference can then be thought of as underlying a deontological distinction between one's duties to *x* and to *y after* they have both been poisoned. It could also lead one to see the failure to provide *x* with an antidote as not exactly or purely an omission.

This whole analysis can then be transposed, *mutatis mutandis*, to our example of promise-breaking. Breaking a promise may involve a less causally immediate or strong relation to harm or loss than what occurs when someone kills or injures someone, but the relation *is* considerably stronger than what occurs when one merely allows another person's promise to go unfulfilled. And as with our poisoning example, there is no reason why someone shouldn't be more sensitive to the fact that if he omits doing something he will have induced someone to incur a loss, than to the fact that if he omits something he will have (merely) allowed someone to incur a loss. This means that in the situation I described one will be more averse to breaking one's promise (by failing to help the promisee in return for what he has already done) than to allowing some other person's promise to be disappointed, and the deontological difference in one's obligations here may thus be accounted for in purely sentimental care-ethical terms. (The very fact that we use the positive-sounding expression 'breaking one's promise' to describe a failure to help in the case we have described may indicate that we see such failure as not a matter purely or exactly of inaction.)

We have so far concentrated on a simple kind of case involving promising: the example we discussed concerned a person who relies on the promise of another and incurs a certain loss by acting first. But (as both MacCormick and Scanlon point out) there are ways one can lose out by relying on a promise, even if one doesn't assume the burden of acting first. Someone who relies on a promise to help may refrain from making other arrangements, for example, from finding someone else who might be willing to help them in exchange for their help, or from finding some other way to accomplish what they want to accomplish. They will then have lost time and opportunities if the promiser doesn't come through for them, and the failure to keep the promise will have the same causal relation to those losses that the failure to help in our first

49

example has to losses that result from actually expending effort and energy. In fact, the earlier example *also* involves opportunity costs, but it should in any event be clear that, even in cases where the promisee doesn't act first, he is likely to incur losses if the promiser is promising falsely or doesn't keep his promise, and a person empathically sensitive to a certain kind of strong causal relation to loss or harm will therefore have a motive for not promising falsely or breaking her promise in such cases. So we can extend our account of what is (deontologically) wrong about breaking promises and making false promises to situations where someone promises to do something in exchange for something else, and then reneges at some later time before either of them has acted.

However, unilateral promises – promises made, as the lawyers say, without consideration – also involve potential costs in opportunities. If I promise to take my teenage son to the theater, then he may not make other plans, and if I at the last minute capriciously decide not to take him, I will be causally responsible for his incurring opportunity costs in a way that my wife, say, will not be. But there is a further problem with breaking a promise (or making a false promise) along these lines. If (as for simplicity we can assume) my son didn't originally expect to go to the theater and regards going to the theater as a special treat, then he wouldn't have been unhappy if the promise had never been made. But if I make the promise and later break it, he will be very disappointed – even apart from his disappointment in *me*. Relying on my promise, he will have confidently anticipated the evening at the theater with pleasure, and it will be very disappointing to find out that he won't in fact be going. (If he assumes a sour-grapes attitude, that might actually show the depth or bitterness of his disappointment.)

Pleasant expectations and confidence about a future good thing are a kind of possession, and to be robbed of them by a promise-breaking is like losing a possession. By contrast, not to have been promised is simply not to have had a certain (psychic) possession, and it is plausible to suppose that the overall experience of the teenager who has been promised an evening at the theater and has had that promise broken is likely to be worse than if he had never been promised in the first place. To be sure, he will have had a certain period of anticipatory pleasure; but the more and the longer he has that pleasure, the worse and the longer he is likely to suffer if his confident expectations are disappointed. This is a familiar fact of human experience, and it adds force to our empathy-related account of the wrongness of breaking a promise to take one's son to the theater.[10] If one breaks one's promise, one will not only have induced one's son to forgo certain prospects or opportunities in a way that one's wife won't have, but will also have induced him to have strong expectations that one then painfully disappointed. The latter fact means that one will have had a causal impact, for the worse, on the quality of one's son's life experiences that one's wife won't have had (even if she could herself have taken the teenager to the theater at the last moment).[11] An empathically caring father has two sorts of reason to avoid falsely promising or breaking a promise to take his son to the theater, and the badness, therefore, of doing such things relates to both the factors we have just discussed. There is potentially similar complexity in the cases discussed earlier.

If I promise someone to help them if they are willing to help me (first), then the promisee may indeed pleasantly anticipate being helped. But because being helped isn't exactly a treat like going to the theater, and because it is easy to focus on the practical aspects of helping and being helped, it is easy (for an abstract philosophical discussion) to ignore the potentially dashed hopes or cruel disappointment suffered by the promisee if one fails to keep one's promise to help him, and to consider mainly his lost practical opportunities and the incurred and uncompensated for costs of his doing his part first, if the promise is broken.

It seems, then, that the notion of disappointing expectations or reliance is actually richer than one might think – and may be ambiguous. When one disappoints expectations, one doesn't do the good or useful thing that a person was expecting, or relying on, one to do, but one also disappoints the person, and disappointment is in itself a bad thing. In cases where one induces someone to believe that one is going to do something they want or value, one hurts the person if one, as we say, lets them down, and this can be true even if the letting down occurs not long after the original promise and before, we can even imagine, the promisee forgoes other opportunities or performs any part of any bargain. Even then the promisee will have lost something good, the confident expectation or assurance that something she wants or values will be done for her; and that is why it is wrong, even in such a case, simply to warn the promisee that one doesn't intend to keep one's promise. But the same obligation to keep a promise won't exist if the thing promised, or threatened, is something the promisee doesn't want, because, aside from the wrongness of making such a threat/promise in the first place, the promisee won't, in the relevant sense, be *disappointed* if one doesn't do what one has said one will.[12] Moreover, a theory that treats the wrong of breaking promises as anchored in the inducing and disappointing of expectations will also want to say that a person isn't morally bound by a promise if she finds out that the promisee, perhaps for good reason, totally distrusts her and has no expectation whatever that she will perform.[13]

Thus the present view handles the same sorts of cases that MacCormick and Scanlon mention, though it invokes considerations of empathy that they never discuss. But I might also point out that nothing any of us says rules out the permissibility of breaking a promise for certain sorts of reasons of self-interest. If someone will die if they pay a visit they have promised to pay, then empathy *vis-à-vis* disappointed expectations is swamped or overcome by fear and prudence, and the person who, in such a case, doesn't pay the promised visit doesn't display a lack of normally developed empathy. Rather, there are natural – built-in, human – limitations to our empathy for others, and the situation just mentioned provides an obvious example of this possibility. By the same token, and for the same reasons we mentioned earlier in connection with killing and harming, empathy can lead one to break a promise if the good to be accomplished by doing so is so great that it outweighs one's empathy-based aversion to having a stronger causal relationship to (or influence on) the lesser losses or evils that will accrue if one breaks the promise. So an ethics of empathic caring needn't treat the obligation to keep promises, or not to make false promises, as absolute. Nor is it forced to regard promising, 'one's word', as sacred or as having force independently of the kinds of considerations we have been speaking of. For example, the fact that I have promised to give you something you are totally indifferent about doesn't necessarily bind me *just because I have promised*. (Scanlon makes similar points.)

Of course, I haven't offered here an account of *what it is* to promise, and despite all the explanations that have been given, I think it is still somewhat mysterious how promising works (to induce expectations). But having said as much, I think it is now finally time to consider truth-telling and lying, which we can do briefly.

There are obviously cases where it isn't wrong to lie; but where it is wrong, our account can cite factors similar to those we have mentioned in our discussion of promising. One can lie about important things, and also about things that a reader or listener has absolutely no practical or other interest in, but even in the latter case there is the possibility, the risk, that the issue one has lied about will affect the interests of the person lied to at some later time, and if the person lied to relies on what one has told her (and assuming, to simplify matters, that what one has told her is in fact false), then the person may be damaged or sustain a loss as a result of relying on what the liar has told her. Perhaps we tend to think of lying as, on the whole or in general, less seriously wrong than breaking promises, because so much lying remains, and is likely to remain, independent of the practical interests of the person lied to, whereas promising and the inducing of reliance typically occur when someone's interests *are* importantly at stake. But in any event, one thing that is wrong with lying is similar to one thing that is wrong with breaking a promise: that one has induced someone to rely on one, to the other person's detriment.

Notice, too, that some lies aren't about the future, much less about some good thing that the person lied to will receive in the future, so their turning out false cannot disappoint expectations in the painful or debilitating way that this can happen with broken promises. This is a further reason for thinking of lying as less serious a wrong than promise-breaking – more kinds of bad things and/or more seriously bad things tend to result from promise-breaking than from lies. Nevertheless, in at least some cases, the wrong one does by lying seems exactly to parallel the wrong one does by breaking a promise.

If someone is going to climb Mount McKinley and I promise to help him make the climb, then, if I don't deliver on my promise, I disappoint him and (presumably worse) I induce him to forgo important opportunities in relation to his climb (or his decision not to climb). But it seems to me that I do something of just the same kind if, instead of promising to do anything for or with the climber, I deceitfully persuade him that another person is going to make the climb with him. Here the lie is just as bad as the breaking of the relevant promise, and that is because the same empathy-eliciting factors are in play in both cases (other things being equal). So there are overall differences between lies and broken (or false) promises, but the ethics of empathic caring can use the same materials it employed to account for the morality of promising to deal with the morality of truth-telling as well.[14]

In our next chapter, I want to begin discussing the notion of respect for other people. It is often said that utilitarianism focuses on concern for others, but cannot make sense of the notion of respect for them, and this is frequently attributed to the fact that utilitarianism also has no room for (the considerations that motivate) deontology. However, we shall see that the emphasis on empathy that helps us make sense of deontology in care-ethical terms likewise allows us to accommodate the idea and ideal of respect for others(' autonomy) in such terms.

Notes

1 My discussion here parallels the criticisms that Shelly Kagan has made of Samuel Scheffler's defense of a morality involving agent-centered permissions or options, but lacking agent-centered restrictions. See Samuel Scheffler, *The Rejection of Consequentialism*, Oxford: Oxford University Press, 1982; Shelly Kagan, 'Does Consequentialism Demand Too Much?', *Philosophy and Public Affairs* 13, 1984, pp. 239–54; and Scheffler's reply to Kagan in the second edition of his book (1994). I think the lesson to be learned from their debate is that partialist views need deontology more than impartialist views do, in order to be at all intuitively plausible – but Kagan and Scheffler were focusing on partiality toward oneself, rather than on the partiality toward near and dear that I have been discussing here.

2 Noddings seems to accept deontology, but doesn't very clearly say *how* an ethics of care can justify deontology (Nel Noddings, *Caring: A Feminine Approach to Ethics and Moral Education*, Berkeley, CA: University of California Press, 1984, pp. 105ff.).

3 For an empirical study indicating that causal immediacy affects empathic/moral reactions in something like the way I have been suggesting, see Michael Koenigs *et al.*, 'Damage to the Prefrontal Cortex Increases Utilitarian Moral Judgements', *Nature*, online version, 21 March 2007. But more studies of the effect of causal factors are needed to complement the many that have already been carried out to show how perception and contemporaneity affect empathy and action.

4 However, I should mention the complicating fact that the distinction between killing and allowing death, and between doing and allowing harm more generally, allows of unclear or controversial cases. See e.g. John Kleinig, 'Good Samaritanism', *Philosophy and Public Affairs* 5, 1975–76, pp. 382–407; Eric Mack, 'Bad Samaritanism and the Causation of Harm', *Philosophy and Public Affairs* 9, 1979–80, pp. 230–59; and Eric Mack, 'Causing and Failing to Prevent', *Southwestern Journal of Philosophy* 7, 1976, pp. 83–90. A completely systematic deontology based on a criterion of empathy would have to sort out such cases.

There are also deontological issues concerning the distinction between harming intentionally (or as a means) and harming as an unintended but foreseen result of what one intentionally does – as, for example, in the famous 'trolley problem'. I believe that our intuitive moral reactions to that case, and to others that have been compared and contrasted with it, reflect felt distinctions of empathy-affecting causal immediacy or directness, and I hope to explore this issue on another occasion. Even if the distinction between doing and allowing is the main issue in or for (the justification of) deontology, I think the notions of empathy and causal immediacy can help us understand other deontological issues as well.

5 These reactions might also vary from person to person, and this might allow a certain vagueness or permissiveness in what an ethics based in the notion of fully developed empathic caring has to say about our moral obligations.

6 In certain sorts of competition, one may intentionally cause someone else to be worse off than they were, or otherwise would have been, without actually *harming* them. A complete ethics of empathy needs to say something about why this kind of causing of bad is morally permissible, but other (more direct, harming) ways of causing bad are not. I am indebted on this point to Stephen Darwall.

7 See N. MacCormick, 'Voluntary Obligations and Normative Powers I', *Proceedings of the Aristotelian Society*, suppl. vol. 46, 1972, pp. 59–78; T. M. Scanlon, *What We Owe to Each Other*, Cambridge, MA: Harvard University Press, 1998, Ch. 7.

8 T. M. Scanlon, *ibid.*, p. 296.

9 Compare and contrast what MacCormick (N. MacCormick, 'Voluntary Obligations and Normative Powers I', *op. cit.*, p. 69) says about the causal difference(s) between disappointing expectations of help that one has induced and simply not helping someone.

10 I hesitate to say that the fact that, for example, we are empathically repelled by active harming is what *makes* such harming wrong, but I do want to say that our present approach seeks to *understand* moral differences by reference to empathy. For the more we see empathy distinctions correlated with the moral ones we are committed to, the more *justified* we are, in any given case, in thinking that a distinction of empathy indicates a valid moral one; and this means that we are able to treat empathy as, at the very least, a criterion of moral acceptability and the like.

11 Here I am of course assuming that the father can be expected to be empathically sensitive to the causal difference between the things he does to his son and what his wife fails to do *for* her son. It is also worth comparing the present argument with what MacCormick says (N. MacCormick, 'Voluntary Obligations and Normative Powers I', *op. cit.*, p. 70) about two kinds of disappointment *vis-à-vis* someone's non-attendance at a dinner.

12 All the considerations just mentioned can be used to help account for what is wrong with breaking one's (unilateral) promise in what Scanlon calls 'the case of the Guilty Secret' (T. M. Scanlon, *What We Owe to Each Other*, *op. cit.*, pp. 302f.). But Scanlon's treatment of the case differs somewhat from what the present approach would say.

13 Compare Scanlon, *ibid.*, pp. 312–14, 405 (note 20); and also Kant's discussion of what would happen if everyone made false promises, in the *Groundwork*, section 2.

14 Hume in the *Treatise* seems not to be explicitly aware of the moral importance of the distinction between doing and allowing, and he never, therefore, focuses on the central deontological issue of killing versus letting die. But he does address the important deontological issues of promise-keeping and respect for property in terms of his theory of the 'artificial' virtues. Hume thinks we can't account for our thinking in this area via 'natural' virtues like benevolence, but if what I have been saying in this chapter is correct, then perhaps we can. Since Hume's theory of artificial virtue is, in important ways, circular (something Hume himself points out), and in other ways quite problematic, our empathy-based account gives moral sentimentalism a second chance, or at least another chance, to try to justify deontology (and to do so in a broader way that takes in the morality of killing and of doing versus allowing).

4

AUTONOMY AND EMPATHY

In this chapter, I want to discuss how an ethics of empathic caring can make sense of the notion of autonomy and of the related notion of respect. Kantians often say that we owe people respect on the basis of their autonomy (or their moral worth or dignity) as rational beings, and so they conceive respect for individuals as respect for their autonomy.[1] But the idea that we owe people respect is broader than the Kantian tradition. It seems *intuitively* plausible to suppose that we ought to respect other people and (also) that we should respect their autonomy, and I think an ethics of care needs to make sense of these notions. But I shall be reversing the Kantian order of explanation. Respect *is* respect for autonomy (or for the capacity for autonomy), and if we can first understand respect, I think we can use that understanding to clarify what autonomy is.

1. Respect

The notions of caring about and concern for (the welfare of) others are widely regarded as different from that of respect. The former are seen as focusing on human (or animal) welfare or wellbeing, the latter seems to invoke or involve some other (distinctive) aspect of human beings, and we see this assumption, for example in *Taking Rights Seriously*, where Ronald Dworkin argues that justice requires the state to treat all its citizens with equal concern *and* respect.[2] Traditional utilitarianism is a welfare-oriented approach to morality, and it has no room for any notion of respect beyond the minimal one of treating all individuals (including animals) the same in consequentialistic welfare calculations. But an ethics of care also focuses on welfare, and so it is natural to think that it has no way of accommodating our intuitive moral thinking about the respect we owe to individuals. And there is also another reason for thinking this.

Care ethics is a form of moral sentimentalism, and it is difficult to see how respect for others can be grounded in (mere) sentiments, emotions, or feelings. I can feel compassion or concern for another person, but these feeling motives seem focused on the other person's welfare, and respect seems, or has been thought, to involve something more or different from any such emotion.

55

Indeed, the fact that respect seems such an intuitive notion with us has been used as an argument against utilitarianism and moral sentimentalism, given the somewhat natural assumption that these approaches can't make sense of what we almost all think about respecting others. But I believe a sentimentalist ethics of care can, in fact, ground respect, and respect for autonomy, in its own terms. Those terms don't, of course, include the Kantian idea that autonomy represents a noumenal feature of human beings. But contemporary Kantian liberals also shy from Kantian metaphysics, so the real issue is whether an ideal of respect that goes beyond (mere, sheer) concern for wellbeing, and that can plausibly be regarded as involving respect *for autonomy*, is derivable from sentimentalist sources.

In the previous chapter we saw that sentimentalism has some perhaps surprising resources for dealing with deontology. In what follows, I hope to show you something similar about respect. Both deontology and respect can, I believe, be conceived and justified by reference to the idea of empathy. And this then leads to a conception of autonomy that likewise falls within the terms and traditions of sentimentalism.

Now this latter point is perhaps no surprise from the standpoint of a sentimentalist ethics of care. Some feminists and/or care-ethicists have developed their own (relational) notion or notions of autonomy to replace what they take to be the more atomistic and putatively less adequate views of autonomy to be found within the (male or masculine) tradition of rationalist/Kantian liberalism. However, in this and the following chapter I shall be going further than other care ethicists have gone. As far as I know, other care ethicists haven't sought to give a theoretical account of respect (for autonomy) in sentimentalist terms, and neither have they explicitly attempted, as I shall be attempting, to *understand (relational) autonomy itself* entirely in care-ethical terms.[3] So I shall end up defending a (relational) conception of autonomy that sits well with the views other care ethicists have about autonomy, but that is more thoroughly grounded in care ethics than those other views have been. However, our first step toward this conclusion requires us to see how respect might be understood in sentimentalist, care-ethical terms.

Concern for wellbeing and respect are often thought to clash when issues of paternalism arise: for example, when someone acts against another person's wishes 'for his or her own good'. Now obviously we all think there are times when paternalism is justified – parents sometimes have to act like parents. But at other times, paternalistic interventions against the expressed wishes or desires of another individual seem morally invidious and unjustified, even though the person who acts in this way can be seen as acting out of caring concern for the wellbeing of the person whose wishes are thwarted. And we typically and intuitively describe what we object to here in terms of respect: we say that the person who intervened showed a lack of respect for the person whose wishes were thwarted, indeed a lack of respect *for their autonomy as individuals*. Here, very roughly, autonomy is regarded as the capacity for making and acting on one's own decisions, and the lack of respect at the very least involves not letting the person exercise that capacity. However, when a *parent* insists, against a child's loudly expressed wishes, on taking that child to the doctor's or dentist's, we *don't* think they are necessarily showing a lack of respect for the child. So what makes the difference?

I believe the most important part of the difference relates to empathy. There is a lack of empathy in most, if not all, cases where a putative concern for wellbeing is accompanied by a failure of respect, and if we enrich the notion of caring so as to make it include empathy, then the ethics of caring will be in a position to account for respect. To see this, we need a more detailed example of how putative concern for wellbeing can involve a lack of respect.

I pointed out earlier that empathy is typically regarded as *not* involving the merging of two souls or personalities. Someone who is overinvolved with another person may have difficulty in separating their own needs and desires from those of the other, and this may mean they fail to respond empathically to what the other needs or wants. One familiar example of such over-involvement can be found in the attitudes some parents have to their children. Parents with a weak sense of self often seek to live through (the successes of) their children, and have a difficult time separating their own needs from those of their children. Such parents *ipso facto* have difficulty empathizing with the individual point of view – the needs, wishes, and fears – of their children. (If the child says they want to do something different from what the parent has planned for them, the parent will often say, and believe, something like 'you don't really want to do that' or 'I know what's best for you, and that isn't it'.) The problem with such parents is not the absence of an emotional connection with their children (they are not like the so-called 'distant father'), but rather *too much connection*. Such overinvolvement or overconnection has recently been labeled 'substitute success syndrome' (henceforward 'sss').[4] And it has been recognized that sss involves an inability to recognize or understand the individuality or wishes of one's children (or others). To that extent, however, it also seems plausible to say that sss parents *fail to respect their children*, since respecting individuals is naturally thought of as requiring respect for their wants and fears and what is individual or distinctive about them.

I am inclined, then, to hold that respect for individuals can be unpacked in terms of empathy. Speaking roughly, one shows respect for someone if, and only if, one exhibits appropriate *empathic* concern for them in one's dealings with them. Furthermore, we saw in particular that sss parents lack empathy for their children's own burgeoning desires and aspirations, and since autonomy – again very roughly – is readily seen as involving a capacity for deciding things on one's own, we can also say that the sss parent shows a lack of respect for their child's nascent *autonomy*. (Or we could say that they show a lack of respect for their child's *capacity* for autonomy. In the present context, it won't make much difference which way one puts it.) In that case, it would appear that a morality of empathic caring requires one to respect other people's autonomy and not just or simply to be concerned with their welfare.[5]

But what is one to say, then, about cases where paternalism is justified, cases, for example, where a parent has to override a child's wishes and entreaties in order to ensure their health? Our theory of respect suggests that such paternalism doesn't show a lack of respect for the child('s autonomy) because the parent in question can be fully empathic with their child's fear of the doctor and nonetheless decide that s/he has to take the child to see the doctor. Such a parent can be visibly upset at what they have to do to their child, and this would show a sensitivity to their child('s point of view) that the sss parent seems to lack. According to the present theory, then, taking one's unwilling child to the doctor needn't show disrespect for the child or for the child's developing autonomy. (I consider issues of paternalism and respect *vis-a-vis* grown-up children and other adults in Chapter 5.)

However, so far we have been basing that theory on one kind of example: cases where parents act, or do not act, respectfully toward their children. It is time to broaden the discussion. A lack of respect can also be shown at the social and/or political level, and the theory I am developing applies very comfortably in this larger sphere. Consider, then, religious autonomy, or freedom of religion.

It is often said that sentiments such as benevolence and love of fellow human beings can motivate people or societies unjustly to *deny* certain people various important forms of religious freedom or liberty and can lead, in effect, to a failure to respect individual and group (rights to) autonomy within the religious sphere. (The same point can be and perhaps has been made about caring.) During the Spanish Inquisition, for example, the religious practices and beliefs of heretics were said to threaten the stability of the state, and it was claimed that the use of torture to force confessions and recantations was necessary to the eternal salvation, and thus to the ultimate wellbeing, of both those with false beliefs and of those who they might corrupt. This is certainly paternalism, and of a kind that most of us find horrifying. But the paternalism here may seem to spring, and is often allowed to have sprung, from good sentiments, and many philosophers and others have argued on that basis that a just social order that respects autonomy and freedom has to go beyond sentiments/ motives like benevolence and concern for others, and acknowledge (on rational grounds) an independent order of rights to various freedoms and liberties.

One can find views like this in J. L. Mackie's *Hume's Moral Theory*[6] and – spelled out at greater length – in Thomas Nagel's *Equality and Partiality*.[7] But in fact I think there is reason to believe that religious intolerance and persecution *don't* arise out of (otherwise admirable) human feelings/motives in the way that Mackie, Nagel, and so many others have assumed. In cases like the Inquisition, the 'dry eyes' (in John Locke's wonderful phrase) of those who persecute and torture others show that such people aren't really concerned about the welfare of those they mistreat, but have other, egotistical or selfish reasons for doing what they do.[8] And this begins, I think, to give us some reason to suspect that we may not need to go beyond sentimentalist considerations and invoke independently justifiable rights to religious freedom and autonomy, in order to explain what is morally repellent and unjust about the denial of religious freedom and autonomy.

However, the main reason for believing this can be stated in terms of empathy. There is something extremely arrogant and dismissive in the attitudes and actions of those who feel they are justified in coercively suppressing the religious beliefs and practices of others. Those who persecute others in this way clearly don't try to understand things from the standpoint of those they persecute, and I think what most strikingly characterizes (arrogant) attitudes and acts of intolerance toward others is a failure to empathize with the point of view of those others.[9] (In the most extreme, but hardly atypical, case, intolerance is accompanied by actual, though perhaps unacknowledged, *hatred* of the other, and hatred is a strong barrier to empathy.) In that case, religious intolerance involves a morally criticizable lack of respect for others that can be understood in terms of an ethics of empathic caring. One needn't go beyond sentimentalism and the sentiments in order to say what is disrespectful, wrong, and unjust about the denial of religious liberty or autonomy.[10]

Now opposition to religious freedom may be compatible with certain kinds and degrees of concern for others, and certainly those who coerce and persecute the adherents of other religions or sects may manage to view themselves as primarily concerned with the welfare of those they coerce and persecute. But the dry eyes make one wonder about egotism, rationalization, and self-deception here, and the concern – even granting that it *is* concern – for those persecuted leads to something that is clearly not morally acceptable. So-called concern for those one persecutes involves, or is accompanied by, an attitude that is arrogantly dismissive of, and lacking in empathy for, the viewpoint of the other. And that is why the idea that empathy is a necessary basis for respect allows us to criticize religious persecution and coercion in care-ethical terms.[11]

2. Autonomy

I would like now to say something more about the nature of autonomy and to do so, as I promised earlier, in the light of what we have just said about respect, which we have understood as equivalent to respect *for* autonomy. Feminists who criticize or condemn (what are considered) male notions of autonomy typically offer a relational theory of autonomy, and the theory I offer is relational in at least one of the senses (see below) that feminists have relied on. But the theory of autonomy I offer is also grounded (entirely) in care ethics, and this is not true of any other relational conception of autonomy that I know of. We have specified respect for autonomy in terms of empathic factors that are absent in sss parents, but present in good or healthy parenting; and we can in the first instance say what autonomy is by claiming that it is what empathic parenting tends to produce and sss parenting tends to preclude.

Think of the sss parent who imposes things on his or her child, and who rides roughshod over the wishes, fears, and desires of that child.[12] If the parent fails to respect those wishes or even to acknowledge them, it will be difficult for the child to accept or acknowledge them too;[13] and it is likely that the child – if not totally and self-thwartingly rebellious – will learn to submit in large part to the authority, the wishes, the priorities, of the parent. Such children will be less likely than others to grow up thinking and deciding things for themselves, and in that case they will lack the kind (or one kind) of autonomy that features centrally in contemporary discussions. In contrast, parents whose empathy with the growing child allows them to care about and encourage the child's maturing aspirations and individuality are showing respect for the child, and such empathy and respect make it more likely that the child *will* grow into an adult who thinks and decides things autonomously. (I am assuming here that rebellion for its own sake doesn't demonstrate autonomy and represents a kind of *negative submission* to actual or displaced parental authority.)

However, I don't want to leave the impression that it is only sss parents who discourage autonomous thinking and aspirations. Many children start to question religious dogmas or rituals, for example, and some (but not all) religious parents strongly discourage such tendencies, making it likely that their children will either accept what their religion tells them 'on faith' or else become rebels against (their) religion. Similarly, sexist attitudes in much of the twentieth century led many parents to discourage their daughters from even considering a career in medicine. If a talented young girl expressed the desire to become a doctor, she would often be told that she 'would really prefer to be a nurse', and such a reply is highly reminiscent of the way sss parents tell their children that they don't *really* want to do certain things (that are inconsistent with what the parent has planned for them). So earlier social mores, attitudes, and institutions can be said to have shown a lack of empathy and respect for the aspirations of many girls; and, as we shall see more clearly in Chapter 6, this represents a form of (sexist) injustice.[14]

What I have just been saying also ties in with some major themes in Carol Gilligan's work. Both in *In a Different Voice* and elsewhere, Gilligan points out that patriarchal societies treat many of the thoughts and aspirations of girls as if they were mistakes or involved misunderstandings.[15] This can lead young girls to doubt or deny their own 'voice', and to a state of dissociation from their own thinking and desires that can result in their being to a substantial extent selfless, self-denying, or self-abnegating – these are all terms she uses – in their relations with others. If this is correct then, making use of our earlier analysis, we can say that selflessness and the like typically result(ed) from the disrespectful way in which some or many girls were or are treated. If it is wrong to treat people with disrespect, then the failure or refusal to listen to what girls say, or see things from their point of view, amounts to wrongdoing (to wronging them); and at the heart of that wrongdoing (or wronging) is a failure of empathy. Gilligan herself doesn't stress empathy or the fact of moral wrongdoing in her discussions of dissociation and selflessness. But once one does, one is in a position to answer the frequently heard criticism that care ethics encourages selfless concern for others and so runs counter to the feminist goal of liberating women from the stereotypical behavior and attitudes that have so disadvantaged them in the past.[16] Perhaps some forms of care ethics do encourage selflessness and self-denial in a retrograde fashion. But a care ethics that is centered around the idea of empathy gives us the tools to make *moral criticisms* of the patriarchal (or other) attitudes and behaviors that have caused many women to value and/or exemplify self-denial and selflessness. This is the very opposite of an encouragement to self-denial and selflessness, and is certainly in keeping with feminist ideals and goals. In Chapter 6, I want to return to this theme as it specifically relates to issues of social justice. But at this point I think we need to go back to our discussion of the nature of autonomy.

I shall be assuming here that autonomy in the sense of thinking and deciding things for oneself is possible in a causally deterministic universe. Of course, autonomy in this sense is, to some extent, a matter of degree, but I do hold, and think it reasonable to hold, that the mere fact that one has been influenced in one's thoughts or decisions does nothing to show a lack or absence of autonomy. Obviously, it can sometimes be reasonable, for example, to take someone's advice, but there is a difference between taking advice and feeling impelled to do or think *whatever* a certain other person or institution tells you to. The former can involve an exercise of autonomy, the latter clearly doesn't. It is very difficult to spell out this distinction in satisfying and complete detail, but this is something philosophers have sought and continue to seek to do, and rather than turn this book into a treatise on the nature of autonomy, I want at this point simply to gesture toward these familiar, though philosophically challenging, distinctions. My purpose here, rather, is to indicate how familiar ideas about autonomy relate to notions like respect, empathy, and caring, and that is what I have just been doing.

Annette Baier tells us that we are all 'second persons', that we have to be a 'you' for some nurturing other before we can be an 'I' for ourselves.[17] This seems obvious once it is stated – though it took a feminist to point it out explicitly for the first time and to point out how that fact seems neglected in traditional liberal/rationalist ('masculine') theories or discussions of autonomy. More significantly, perhaps, the fact that we are originally second persons indicates that autonomy is, at the very least, *causally* relational. But the present attempt to understand autonomy by reference to respect and caring fills out the idea of relational autonomy in a very specific way. Our account says that such autonomy is just what respect for autonomy – understood as involving empathic care or caring – *tends to produce*.

Now autonomy, as the developed and exercised capacity to think and decide things for oneself, is pretty clearly good for people. To be sure, it can be difficult and even painful to think and act autonomously, and if we took a very crude (and short-sighted) hedonistic view of how human beings flourish, autonomy might seem problematic. But despite all the problems that can accompany autonomy (and that can lead some people to attempt to 'escape from freedom'), it still seems to most of us, intuitively, to be a highly desirable state; and its status as such has been defended by many philosophers, myself included.[18] So I think we should assume here that autonomy is an important human good. In that case, our care ethics treats respectful, empathic caring both as morally incumbent on parents, and as the likeliest way to produce the highly desirable state of autonomy. But think too about what autonomy *involves*. We have argued that autonomy is inconsistent with selflessness, and that means that the autonomous person can recognize, and isn't afraid of, his or her own desires or aspirations. This, too, is a desirable state for a person to be in;[19] and that means, I think, that we are now in a position to expand usefully on Baier's idea that we are, and have to be, second persons before we become first persons. What in fact emerges from our previous discussion is the more specifically (or explicitly) ethical conclusion that it is by being initially *treated well as second persons* that we become likely or more likely to *do well as first persons*.

Now the kind of autonomy we have been focusing on involves the realization of the initial human capacity for thinking and deciding things for oneself. I have sometimes slipped in what I hope are harmless ways between references to autonomy as a developed or realized capacity, and references to it as the/an exercise of that capacity. And there is also autonomy as a basic human capacity that needs to be developed and that it is desirable to exercise. Still, all these references are to a form of autonomy that is seen as lying within given individuals, and as relational only in the sense of having been or needing to be brought about by other individuals (operating in a given society and environment). Feminist relational autonomy is frequently understood in such causal terms, but sometimes autonomy is said (also) to be *constitutively* relational.[20] What does this mean, and how does it fit in with what we have been saying up to this point?

Those who say that autonomy is constitutively relational often cite the fact that our exercise of autonomy requires 'cooperating' institutions and social attitudes.[21] Even a woman who is intent on becoming a doctor cannot fulfill her ambition unless some medical school is willing to accept her as a student. So in this case, and others, the successful exercise of autonomy would appear to depend on external factors; and those factors can seem more like constitutive conditions than like causes of exercising autonomy. This conclusion may be correct, but what is at work here might also be an ambiguity in the notion of autonomy as between an (exercised) internal capacity for making one's own decisions and the absence of external factors that interfere with one doing what one wants.

When a region in a given country is autonomous, the country (as a matter of law) doesn't interfere in or with various of the region's activities, and religious autonomy is also naturally regarded as an absence of interference with the exercise of religious freedom (on the part of the state or certain people). But individuals may be free from outside interference at a given time without having the capacity to think or decide things for themselves. The state and its citizens may not interfere with religious liberty, but religious individuals may, nonetheless, have an entirely submissive attitude to what their parents or church have taught them. In that case, the religious people fail to be autonomous in the sense we have been working with so far, but they do have another kind of autonomy, the kind that involves an absence of outside interference (and that we sometimes attribute, on a larger scale, to regions or provinces in a given country, etc.). This latter kind of autonomy, moreover, appears to be constitutively, and not just causally, relational, because freedom from outside interference seems to just *be* the absence of certain external factors and activities.

We need to say a bit more about this constitutively relational kind of autonomy, and we shall do so in Chapter 6, below. But for the moment let me point out that interference with an individual's autonomy seems, morally at least, to require some sort of justification, and mention that Chapter 6 will have something substantial to say about when such interference is just or morally acceptable. We have already seen that interference with the free exercise of religion constitutes disrespect and can be condemned as unjust, but Chapter 6 will need to expand on this idea and offer a general criterion of when interference with liberty is unjust and when it isn't.

Before we get to Chapter 6, however, we still have important work to do on the notion of autonomy. I have talked about autonomy and respect for it in terms of empathy and empathic concern or caring, and what we have had to say has so far yielded some fairly intuitive conclusions. But there is a more traditional, rationalistic notion of autonomy embodied in the liberal Kantian tradition, and it is imperative that we now understand how and why these two views of autonomy differ. Care ethics is certainly free to offer its own conception of autonomy and respect (for autonomy); but the question then arises whether that conception is as plausible, all things considered, as the traditional view. Nor have we yet focused entirely on questions about individual or social *rights* of autonomy or non-interference, but in the next chapter such questions will occupy center stage. It will turn out that the whole issue between the liberal and care-ethical views of respect for autonomy concerns when it is right (or just) to interfere with autonomous individual choices, and when individuals have a moral right *against* such interference.

Now one might imagine at this point that these issues about interference center around paternalistic examples, with care ethics allowing for and mandating a caring paternalism in various cases where a liberal would regard paternalistic intervention as violating someone's right not to be interfered with. But for reasons I shall make apparent later in Chapter 5, liberalism and care ethics may differ less about paternalistic interventions than one might (and I did) initially think. Instead, and as I shall argue early in Chapter 5, the real crux of disagreement between them concerns cases where a person may want to interfere with someone else's activities in order to prevent *third parties* from being harmed.

Notes

1 I shall focus mainly on respect for autonomy and autonomy itself, leaving dignity and worth pretty much to themselves. But I assume that if the former notions can be accounted for, the latter are either inessential or can be explained in similar terms. (See reference to Seyla Benhabib in note 5.)

2 Ronald Dworkin, *Taking Rights Seriously*, London: Duckworth, 1978, pp. 180–83, 272–78.

3 Jennifer Nedelsky, 'Reconceiving Autonomy: Sources, Thoughts and Possibilities' (*Yale Journal for Law and Feminism* 1, 1989, pp. 7–36) offers a ground-breaking defense of relational autonomy that seeks to model such autonomy on the mother–child relationship. But even though Nedelsky's piece shows the influence of care ethics, it doesn't explicitly espouse an ethics of care or (therefore) attempt to integrate relational autonomy into such an ethics; neither does it tie relational autonomy to empathy or respect. These are all things I shall be doing here. Grace Clement (*Care, Autonomy, and Justice: Feminism and the Ethics of Care*, Boulder, CO: Westview Press, 1996, Ch. 2) anticipates the present book in stressing the importance of (empathic) parental caring to the development of relational autonomy, but makes the further claim that autonomy *cannot* be entirely understood in care-ethical terms. Clement holds that the ethics of justice (conceived separately from caring) is also essential to understanding autonomy, and that is just what I am going to be denying here.

4 On substitute success syndrome, see L. Blum, M. Homiak, J. Housman and N. Scheman, 'Altruism and Women's Oppression' in C. Gould and M. Wartofsky, eds, *Women and Philosophy*, New York: Putnam, 1976, esp. p. 238. And for helpful relevant discussion, also see Clement, *ibid.*

5 Seyla Benhabib, 'The Generalized and the Concrete Other: The Kohlberg–Gilligan Controversy and Feminist Theory' (in S. Benhabib and D. Cornell, eds, *Feminism as Critique: On the Politics of Gender*, Minneapolis, MN: University of Minnesota Press, 1987, esp. pp. 89–82) argues that recognizing the dignity of the 'generalized other' necessitates seeing things from the standpoint of the 'concrete other'. This comes very close to the view I am defending here, and there are also similarities between what I am saying and Nancy Sherman's 'Concrete Kantian Respect', *Social Philosophy and Policy* 15, 1996, pp. 119–48.

Finally, I assumed at certain points in the text (though not at others) that it is possible to be genuinely concerned about another's welfare *without* taking up their point of view or respecting their autonomy, but that was a concession made, basically, for expository purposes. I mention some strong reasons for questioning (or qualifying) it in Michael Slote, *Morals from Motives*, New York: Oxford University Press, 2001, esp. pp. 131f.

6 J. L. Mackie, *Hume's Moral Theory*, London: Routledge & Kegan Paul, 1980, p. 28.

7 Thomas Nagel, *Equality and Partiality*, New York: Oxford University Press, 1991, pp. 154–68.

8 See Locke's *Second Essay on Government* in *Two Essays on Government*, ed. Peter Laslett, Cambridge: Cambridge University Press, 1960. Notice the contrast here with the empathic parent who is *upset* at having to take his or her unwilling child to the doctor's or dentist's.

9 Marilyn Friedman has pointed out to me that a torturer may need to understand her/his victim's feelings and reactions in order to be able to really hurt the victim; by the

same token, it is often said that psychopaths can understand what makes people tick with exquisite precision, and that this is precisely what enables them to use or abuse unsuspecting victims. But a cold and sadistic/manipulative understanding is not the same thing as empathy, and it is generally agreed that psychopaths lack empathy for *anyone*. Likewise, those who torture classes of victims who they hate or condemn arguably don't (fully or substantially) empathize with those victims – but more needs to be said about this.

10 Since empathy is, and is supposed to be, more strongly evoked toward people one personally knows, the empathic concern that constitutes respect for (the autonomy of) fellow citizens or compatriots will tend to be less than what is necessary to respect for (the autonomy of) one's own children. Still, our empathy for compatriots who adhere to a different religion can easily be strong enough to allow us to understand religious matters from their point of view and be tolerant of their beliefs and customs; and that seems all that respect requires, in this instance. Our theory entails that what respect for someone requires depends both on that individual's particular needs and desires, and on one's particular *relation or connection* to that individual, but although this may not be typical of views about respect, its implications seem quite plausible.

Let me at this point also quickly add that since (even) *tolerance* can sometimes coexist with hatred, one shouldn't put too much weight on that notion in describing the attitudes and actions characteristic of empathic respect for others. (I am indebted here to Susan Brison.)

11 In *Morals from Motives, op. cit.*, Ch. 5, I describe a science-fiction case in which a refusal to grant certain religious liberties would be justified and in no way demonstrate a lack of empathy. But it is difficult to think of a single case in actual human history where religious persecutions or intolerance *didn't* reflect a failure of empathy. So if we wish to defend religious liberties in the circumstances of actual human life, our sentimentalist approach may give us all we need. (For further discussion of the idea that religious persecutions and intolerance reflect a lack of empathy toward 'out-group members', see Albert Bandura, 'Reflexive Empathy: On Predicting More Than One Has Ever Observed', *Behavioral and Brain Sciences* 25, 2002, pp. 24f.)

12 Much of what I am saying also applies to parental substitutes who may be raising a child.

13 Since the notion of empathy for oneself is somewhat strained (unless, perhaps, we are talking about one's much earlier or much later self), I don't propose to understand self-respect in terms of empathy. Rather, given the account offered above, the conditions of self-respect may turn out pretty much to be the conditions of autonomy itself. A failure of parental respect undermines both the child's (progressive realization of the capacity for) autonomy and the child's earlier and later self-respect. But perhaps it is most accurate to say that self-respect involves a sense of the importance of one's own aspirations and beliefs and that autonomy, in the sense of actually deciding things for oneself, causally depends on such a sense of self-respect.

14 My sketchy account of the causal origins of autonomy tends to support what Natalie Stoljar calls the 'feminist intuition' that 'preferences influenced by oppressive norms of femininity cannot be autonomous' – that a fully autonomous individual doesn't have such preferences. In the light of my discussion of respect and empathy, the example of the young girl who is taught/forced to think she has to become a nurse rather than a doctor in fact illustrates *how* the influence of oppressive social norms of femininity can undermine autonomy. See Stoljar's 'Autonomy and the Feminist Intuition' in C. MacKenzie and N. Stoljar, eds, *Relational Autonomy: Feminist*

Perspectives on Autonomy, Agency, and the Social Self, New York: Oxford University Press, 2000, esp. p. 95.

15 See Carol Gilligan, *In a Different Voice: Psychological Theory and Women's Development*, Cambridge, MA: Harvard University Press, 1982, Ch. 3; Carol Gilligan, 'Hearing the Difference: Theorizing Connection' in *Anuario de Psicologia* 34, 2003, pp. 155–61.

16 For an example of such criticism see Martha Nussbaum, *Sex and Social Justice*, New York: Oxford University Press, 1999, pp. 74ff. Gilligan offers her own kind of answer to this criticism in 'Hearing the difference ...'; in 'Reply by Carol Gilligan', *Signs* 11, 1986, pp.324–33; and, originally, in *In a Different Voice, ibid.*, Ch. 3.

17 Annette Baier, 'Cartesian Persons' in her *Postures of the Mind: Essays on Mind and Morals*, Minneapolis, MN: University of Minnesota Press, 1985, pp. 84ff.

18 For defense of the personal desirability of autonomy, see e.g. Brad Hooker's 'Is Moral Virtue a Benefit to the Agent?' (in R. Crisp, ed., *How Should One Live?*, Oxford: Clarendon Press, 1996, esp. p. 145); and Michael Slote, *Morals from Motives* (New York: Oxford University Press, 2001, Ch. 8).

19 But the fact that autonomy is desirable for individuals in these ways doesn't in any way imply that the autonomous person has to be lacking in empathy. As explained in Chapter 2 (note 29), the effectiveness of inductive discipline may depend on, and is certainly enhanced by, the fact that the parent who calls a child's attention to the pain or harm that child has caused, and who does so in order to prevent the child from causing similar pain or harm in the future, *is exhibiting empathy*. Thus really empathic parents can both instill empathic concern for others – and at the same time nurture autonomy and a lack of selflessness – in their children.

20 For various views of the relationality of autonomy, see the essays collected in C. MacKenzie and N. Stoljar, eds, *Relational Autonomy, op. cit.*

21 See, for example, Jennifer Nedelsky, 'Reconceiving Autonomy: Sources, Thoughts and Possibilities', *op. cit.*; Marina Oshana, 'Personal Autonomy and Society', *Journal of Social Philosophy* 29, 1998, pp. 81–102.

5

CARE ETHICS VERSUS LIBERALISM

1. Defining the Issues

Many feminists and care ethicists have sought to understand autonomy in non-traditional terms, stressing the relational character of individual human autonomy in a way that standard liberals or Kantians have never done. (Contemporary liberals may not want to *deny* that autonomy is causally relational, that an ability to think and decide for oneself at least partly depends on how we have interacted with others and the world in general. But liberalism and Kantianism have certainly tended to ignore or downplay this fact.) However, those who have proposed an alternative, relational view of autonomy haven't attempted to integrate such a view completely into the ethics of caring. To be sure, the ethics of care stresses connection and relationship, and this sits well with the idea that autonomy should be conceived in relational terms. But liberals think our autonomy should be respected, and a care ethics that takes autonomy seriously needs to say something substantive about respect, and about respect for autonomy in particular. This has not, to the best of my knowledge, been done previously, but in the previous chapter I attempted to show how the notion of empathy helps us to integrate both autonomy and respect for autonomy into a comprehensive ethics of care.

However, the liberal or Kantian views respect for autonomy very differently from the way our ethics of empathic care sees it. The liberal sees respect for an individual's autonomy as involving the recognition of a wide range of individual rights against non-interference by others, and an ethics of care will be inclined to deny (what the liberal takes to be) some of the most important of those rights. In this area, as we shall see, liberalism and anything that looks like a care-ethical approach will hold inconsistent views about particular cases, and so I am hoping now to deliver on my earlier promise to show that and why 'justice thinking', as typified by liberalism, and 'care thinking', as exemplified in an ethics of care, cannot be harmonized or integrated. We can't avoid choosing between caring and justice, and I shall be arguing in what follows that there is some reason to prefer an ethic of caring.

Kantian liberals believe in broad rights of free speech (and assembly). They tend to hold that it is wrong to prevent or interfere with freedom of speech, even if doing so is or would be necessary to protect (a large number of) people from harm; and many of them – for example, Ronald Dworkin, Thomas Scanlon, and Thomas Nagel – appeal to (facts about) human autonomy as their basis for making such claims.[1] But many feminists (and others) disagree with these views. They object to various forms of 'hate speech' and so recognize a narrower right of non-interference (with free speech) than what liberalism subscribes to.[2] The two sides disagree, for example, about whether the neo-Nazi march in Skokie, Illinois (which never actually occurred) should have been permitted, despite all the suffering it would or could have caused to Holocaust survivors who lived in that town.[3] And I think a developed ethics of care will definitely side against the liberal on this question. The main issue for such an ethics will be the considerable harm that hate speech can cause, rather than the interference with the freedom or autonomy of those who wish to give vent to hate speech, and I shall make this point clearer in what follows.

Now the Skokie case, and others like it, involve issues of jurisprudence, but it is easy enough, I think, to invent more personal or individual situations where there is no question of making, or changing, or adjudicating a law, but where the same division of opinion and the same reasons for the division exist. Thus consider a woman whose father is a neo-Nazi leader and who lives in a town where permission for a neo-Nazi parade and speeches has been granted. If she temporarily hides his false teeth (or his toupee), he will be too embarrassed to take part in the march and the speeches and (let us assume) the whole thing will collapse, saving a large number of Holocaust survivors a great deal of pain. In the light of what we know about differing reactions to the idea of hate speech legislation, it seems likely that there will be a difference of opinion about whether it is wrong of her to hide the false teeth (or toupee) and interfere with the father's right of free speech.

Once again, moreover, the care ethicist who emphasizes empathy will be more likely than the liberal to find such individual action morally permissible. We may have a moral obligation to respect the autonomy of others, but the account offered in the previous chapter understood such respect as coming down to empathically sensitive concern for others, and the daughter may have such concern both for her father and for those whom his hate speech will likely hurt. She rejects her father's political views and is acutely aware, let us imagine, of what it must be like for a survivor to be reminded of the Holocaust in such an obtrusive or shocking way. But she also loves her father and understands very well how important his Nazism is to his (view of his own) life. Having to choose between the survivors and her father, she thinks more serious and greater damage will be caused to the former, if she lets him find his toupee or false teeth, than will be caused to the latter (together with other neo-Nazis), if she hides it/them. In other cases, where one has to choose between individuals or groups of individuals, a choice in one direction needn't entail a lack of empathy in the other – if I can adopt only one orphan from an orphanage, I may be acutely and empathically aware of the (hurt) feelings of a particular orphan I decide not to adopt. And by the same token there may be no failure of empathy on the part of the neo-Nazi's daughter: she may be quite sensitive to the frustration her father and/or the other neo-Nazis will feel or are feeling. So the ethics of empathic care will hold that she shows no lack of respect for anyone if and when she decides to hide her father's toupee or teeth; and it views such an action as morally permissible.[4]

By contrast, the liberal notion of respect for autonomy treats such respect as requiring that one honor an individual's (independently justifiable) right to speak his or her mind, despite the damage this is likely to cause to people's psychological wellbeing. It insists on the wrongness of interfering with individual liberties across a broader range of examples and issues than can be justified in terms of an ethics of empathic care. And in insisting on a larger or broader right of autonomy, it stresses autonomy and rights in just the way that Carol Gilligan and others have said is typical of traditional male moral thinking. This difference between two voices, between care thinking and traditional justice thinking, can be illustrated both by political/jurisprudential and by individual/personal examples, and the most important immediate conclusion seems to me to be the fact that the two forms of thought – the (liberal) ethics of justice and the ethics of caring – are inconsistent with one another.

But even assuming that we have to choose between them, we have not, so far, been given any reason to prefer a (generalized) caring approach. That is something I shall try to do later in this chapter, but first it is important to become clearer on some further issues concerning gender and moral thinking. It is time to discuss the work of psychoanalyst Nancy Chodorow, whose views about the nature and results of traditional child-rearing greatly influenced Gilligan's conclusion (in *In a Different Voice*) that men and women tend, on the whole, to think differently about morality.[5] As I mentioned in the Introduction, many psychologists and educationists have questioned this conclusion. So it might well be wondered why I haven't questioned it myself, and I want to consider this issue now in relation to Chodorow's ideas.

Chodorow's *The Reproduction of Mothering* offers a potential explanation of why (educated, Western, middle-class) women might tend to think about moral issues in terms of caring about and connection with others, and why (similarly characterized) men might tend to think about such issues in terms of traditionally conceived justice, autonomy, and rights. She argues that traditional child-rearing practices make it understandable that women should value connection and men should, to some extent, fear it and value autonomy or separateness from others instead. Boys and girls, in the past and even today, are primarily raised by their mothers, and that means girls can get a pretty full sense of their gender identity at home. But boys have to break away from mother and home if they want to join the world of men('s activities and accomplishments) and learn to identify with what men do and are. To the extent that it is tempting to stay comfortably tied to one's mother, but a boy feels a stronger need or impulsion to become the man that (everyone says) he is supposed to become, a fear of too much connection and a high valuing of separateness are likely to emerge, which is just what the different voices hypothesis suggests. This explanation seems capable of accounting for the fact (if it is one) that men and women tend to think differently about morality.[6] But nothing in Chodorow's views or present evidence rules out the possibility that, with more 'egalitarian' child-rearing practices, men and women might become more alike in their thinking. To believe that there are differences between men and women as they are at present needn't commit us to gender essentialism, and Chodorow herself argues against such essentialism in her book.[7]

However, in an article entitled 'Moral Orientation and Moral Development', which was published some years after In a Different Voice, Gilligan describes her findings about male/female differences in a way that I believe calls Chodorow's explanation into question.[8] When one confines one's attention to the educated, middle class, Western, etc., individuals that most research has focused on, it turns out that many women think in terms of justice – just about as many as think in terms of caring. Gilligan makes it clear, on the other hand, that almost no (such) men think in terms of caring; but what she is saying about women's thinking seriously threatens Chodorow's explanation of male and female differences.[9] If many women think in terms of traditional autonomy and justice, then the explanation of such thinking can't simply be put in terms of the male need to identify with a father who is more absent from the home than his mother is. Similarly, the explanation of why women think in terms of caring can't simply be that the mother girls are supposed to identify with is in the home and intimately connected with them. That wouldn't explain why so many girls who are (presumably, or as far as Chodorow shows) in the same position actually favor justice thinking. So I don't believe we can use Chodorow's ideas as Gilligan originally intended, and we perhaps have (even) more reason than previously to doubt the correlation between gender (or sex) and moral voice or orientation.[10]

Thus care thinking may, at this point, be almost exclusively a female phenomenon; but justice thinking is widespread among women, and it is a mistake or exaggeration to think of liberalism, for example, as a (primarily) male or masculine approach to moral/political issues. Many women defend liberalism and/or argue for permitting hate speech on the basis of the autonomy considerations that liberalism appeals to;[11] and that is why in the present chapter I have avoided characterizing the opposed views I have been speaking of as either masculine/male or feminine/female. But we certainly can say that care ethics and Kantian liberalism take opposing views of our autonomy rights of free speech, as exemplified in the issue of hate speech; and if we want to defend the ethics of care, we need to defend its approach to that issue and/or others over that taken by the liberal.

However, there is another question that I think we need to address before we consider whether care ethics is superior to liberalism. The ethics of care may not be properly characterizable as the ethics of women, but my particular development of care ethics stresses empathy, and arguably women are, on the whole or on average, more empathic than men. This is something Chodorow asserts in her book;[12] but it is also something for which there seems to be a great deal of (independent) evidence.[13] And if women are more empathic than men, and we accept a care ethics that give empathy a central place, this may give us a reason to say that women are, at least at present, morally superior to men. Is that something we – both men and women – can live with?

In a Different Voice argues that we should think of the female moral voice as different from, rather than inferior to, that of males; and in the original version of the book there is no hint (that I can detect) that the female voice should actually be thought of as superior. But that thought is, at the very least, suggested in the 'Letter to Readers, 1993' that is included as a preface to later printings of the book, which asks (pp. xxvi–xxvii) whether the traditional (male) voice of separateness can't, won't, or shouldn't 'give way' to a new (and female) way of thinking that puts a greater value on relationship and connection. (The epigram at the beginning of the present book comes from this passage.) At any rate, in other work Gilligan seems quite comfortable with the idea that the voice of caring and connection, which is almost exclusively to be found among women, is morally preferable to the voice of justice and autonomy as traditionally understood.[14] But not every advocate of care ethics has felt this way. Lawrence Blum seems to think it makes sense to resist the idea that either sex/gender is morally superior to the other,[15] and for the longest time – perhaps because I am a male – I too found myself resisting this conclusion. However, I am no longer convinced that I/we should.

In the first place, if we really assume that women are more empathic than men, then we probably have to assume that men are, on average, more adept than women at making and following rules or universal principles. So Kantian liberalism – with its stress on rules, principles, laws – may have to say that men are morally superior to women. (This is something Kant himself was willing to claim.)[16] So if our main theoretical choice in ethics is between liberalism and care ethics, then we may be unable to avoid saying that *one* sex/gender is superior to the other (or another). The question would then be: which theory, liberalism or care ethics, gives a better account of ethical phenomena? And the way one answered that question would determine which sex/gender was superior.

But this does risk turning moral theory into another instance of the war of the sexes, and if one then argued for the preferability of care ethics, as I shall be doing very explicitly later in this chapter, one would be committed to the (at least present-day) moral superiority of women in a way that men might well find offensive. Wouldn't that make it difficult for care ethics to serve as a morality for all human beings, and wouldn't it, therefore, in one way or another give us – both men and women – a reason to doubt the validity of care ethics (or Kantian ethics) as a comprehensive (human) account of morality? I am not, in fact, sure.

In the first place, the overall difference in empathic tendencies between men and women might be due largely to differences in the way men and women have been raised, socialized, or educated.[17] [18] If empathy is primarily shaped by practices of child-rearing and socialization, then different practices could lead to men becoming much more empathic than they are, on the whole, nowadays. In particular, if we adopted a care-ethical approach to our social practices and institutions, we could encourage/educate *everyone* to be empathically caring in relation to others, and male displays of emotion, nurturing, and altruism generally wouldn't be devalued or looked down on (by males) in the way they tend to be at present.[19] (In the past 40 years, society has already moved in this direction to a considerable extent.) These changes would presumably lead men to be much more empathic and caring (and more involved, for example, in child-rearing) than they are, on the whole, at present. But would they, could they, entirely close the 'morality gap' that (according to care ethics) exists between men and women?

Quite possibly not. A good deal of the evidence concerning the greater empathic tendencies of girls and women derives from studies indicating that having, at various stages, higher levels of testosterone makes boys and men more aggressive and less socially perceptive and empathic than girls and women. (Aggressiveness and empathic openness to the needs/feelings of others do seem like contrary character traits.) There is a large and growing literature on this subject,[20] and it seems to give us reason to hold that there will inevitably be differences in men's and women's empathicness, even if we do all we can to change social practices and attitudes in accordance with care-ethical (or any other) moral ideals or standards. An advocate of care ethics (along the lines of the present book) would then, presumably, have to agree/admit that, in the sphere of morality, women are *basically* superior to men, and we can ask once again: Is this something men can or could find acceptable? More particularly, could a man reasonably and willingly admit that, for reasons having to do with (their higher levels of) testosterone, men are fundamentally and on the whole less morally capable than women?

Well, consider this. Even if men are less empathic than women, present-day men can be very empathic, and no one has suggested that altered educational/child-rearing practices couldn't render men much more empathic, on the whole, than they are at present. (And no-one denies that women could become more empathic, on the whole, than *they* are at present.) So consider a man who is capable of considerable empathy and ask him what he thinks about the way testosterone undercuts empathy in men and invariably makes them, as a sex or gender, more aggressive toward others than women tend to be. Wouldn't he be likely to deplore and regret these effects of testosterone precisely because of the empathy and empathic concern he feels for those whom testosterone-influenced aggression has harmed or hurt? It seems to me that any sufficiently empathic male/man *would* feel regret or even guilt about these effects of male testosterone, and if he does, then at that point he seems to have no basis or motive for resisting or resenting the idea that men are morally inferior to women. That conclusion may constitute a kind of blow or buffet to the ego, but for someone who recognizes and deplores the damage that results from superabundant male testosterone, it may be a buffet one feels one has to accept.

Moreover, the acceptance of moral inferiority may carry with it certain advantages or benefits. If, as suggested above, men are less morally capable than women, then that very fact may give men some sort of moral excuse when their testosterone leads them to act badly or less well than they otherwise might. The literature on testosterone and human behavior indicates that autistic (including Asperger's syndrome) males are incapable of empathy and have even higher testosterone levels than typical males. Since we are inclined to excuse the moral failings of austistic people, don't we then have reason, though to a lesser extent, to excuse the moral failings of men generally?[21] If we do, an ethics of care might hold men to be less morally responsible or accountable than women. When men performed certain aggressive acts, or were in certain ways empathically insensitive to the needs of others, the theory could say that what they had done was morally wrong, but to some degree excusable; and this gives men a kind of moral excuse that the theory denies to women. At that point, it is women who would be more likely to object to an ethics of care, and it seems, more generally, that both men and women could have grounds – though of very different kinds – for resenting or rejecting care ethics. Men can mind being regarded as morally inferior to women; women can mind being held more accountable for their actions than men. But on the other hand, men who were sensitive enough to regret and deplore the damage their increased testosterone levels had led men to cause or allow might feel relieved to learn that their testosterone gave them some kind of moral excuse for their behavior. Likewise, women who suspected that care ethics was letting men off too easily might, nonetheless, take pride in the thought that, because of their greater empathic capacities and lesser aggressive tendencies, they were morally superior to men and had less need of the moral excuses men have to rely on.[22]

I therefore think that an ethics of care that centers around empathy needn't feel too uncomfortable with the idea that women are now, and are likely to remain, morally superior to men; and the acceptance of that conclusion doesn't in any way debar care ethics from functioning as a moral standard or ideal for both men and women.[23] It also doesn't have to prevent care ethics from having a helpful role in bringing about appropriate and needed changes in present-day practices, customs, institutions, and attitudes. But it is time now (finally) to consider some of the arguments that might be, or have been, given to show the superiority, not of women to men, but of care ethics to liberalism. Most of those arguments are not, in the end, very strong, but one of them, I think, does offer us some reason to reject liberalism in favor of an approach like the present one. After discussing that argument, I want to change the subject to paternalism, and in the final section of this chapter we shall see that liberalism and care ethics may very well not be as divergent in their views about paternalism as one might initially imagine.

2. Arguments against Liberalism

In A *Theory of Justice*, the great liberal political thinker John Rawls claimed that ethical theories ought to take into account and reflect the metaphysical nature(s) of the individuals they are intended to apply to (and guide).[24] Rawls used this idea to criticize utilitarianism, a view that is historically rooted in sentimentalism and that still bears many of the marks of its origins. But care ethicists, feminists, and also communitarians have sought to turn this sort of argument on its head by showing that it is liberals like Rawls, Nagel, and others who misconceive the metaphysical nature of the selves, the persons, to whom (political) morality is supposed to apply. They have argued that personal identity, or persons, are essentially or constitutively relational and that liberals and Kantians assume a falsely atomistic picture of our identity.[25] We need to consider how strongly this criticism affects the prospects of liberalism.

An atomistic view of the self, or of persons, is one that sees relations or relationships with other persons as non-essential to the identity of the person who has such relations or relationships. Kant's noumenal view of the self is clearly atomistic in this sense, but even liberals who don't subscribe to Kantian metaphysics often have an atomistic view in the above sense. For example, Rawls, in A *Theory of Justice*, says that our nature is revealed not by our aims, but by the principles of right and justice that govern how these aims are to be formed and pursued. The self, he holds, is prior to its ends, and its essential unity requires nothing more than our understanding of and commitment to what is morally right. So it is only our rational/critical/moral capacities themselves that need to remain in place in order for basic identity to be retained through changes in who we love and what we want.[26] Other liberals say similar things, and one can find such views very usefully catalogued (and extensively criticized) in Michael Sandel's *Liberalism and the Limits of Justice*.[27] But note one thing: the liberal atomist needn't, and doesn't, say that selves are bare (personal/rational) particulars without social or interpersonal characteristics. They think our commitments and relationships *do* characterize us, but also hold that even the most important ties to others are not essential to, or definitive of, our identity.

Now of course the feminist or communitarian needn't, and typically doesn't, hold that all our commitments and relationships are essential to us. Presumably, only the most important of these can constitute, or be part of what constitutes, the identity of any given person, and it is typically examples such as close family or personal relationships (parenthood, friendships, marriages) and like commitments to a large cause or community (for example to the Jewish community, or to the cause of feminism) that are mentioned as essential constituents of individual identity. But what does it mean to say that such commitments and relationships are essential to, and not just features of, a person?

In Anglo-American philosophy, at least, the *locus classicus* of discussion of what is essential and what is accidental to individuals (or other 'entities') is Saul Kripke's *Naming and Necessity*.[28] Kripke uses the notion of essential properties that is tied to possible worlds: a property is essential to me (roughly) if I have it in every possible world where I exist, and possible worlds (again, roughly) are worlds that can be distinctly conceived and imagined, even if, for example, they violate the physical laws or historical facts of the actual world. Kripke argues, for example, that our origins are essential to us: if I came from particular parents and from a particular sperm and egg, then there is no possible world in which a person emerges from a *different* sperm and egg or *different* parents and is really *me*. But on Kripke's view, the fact that I go to college, or have the spouse, children, or friends that I do, is not essential to me; similarly, it is only my origination from my parents that counts as essential to me, not the fact, if it is one, that I love them and see them as important to my life.

To be sure, and assuming the above facts, I would be a (very) different person if I didn't love them or have the other personal relationships that are important to me, but I wouldn't be *another* person, if I irrationally or immorally turned against my parents, friends, children, spouse and abandoned them all for other relationships or to become a hermit. The person we are imagining doing all these things is still *me rather than another person*. And so, for Kripke, relationships in the personal, as opposed to the biological, sense are not essential, and if we accept Kripke's views – and almost everyone who is willing to accept the metaphysical idea of essential properties has by and large agreed with what Kripke says about these matters – then the individual atomism of liberal political philosophers may not involve an error about the nature of persons. As far as I know, no feminist or communitarian has directly engaged Kripke's arguments, but it seems to me that is precisely what is needed if one is to claim that liberal political and moral views – and the liberal view, in particular, of freedom of speech – are based on a faulty conception of human identity and personhood.

However, before we leave this question, let me mention one possible reply that might occur to the feminist or communitarian. It could be said that Kripke's notion of essential properties is a strictly logical one, and that the difference between what is essential or constitutive of identity and what merely or accidentally characterizes a given individual is more profitably regarded as a difference, in less logical and more human terms, between what is important and what is not really important to a given individual's being what s/he is. Such a reply is plausible and attractive, but I wonder if (without a great deal of further elaboration) it has much force against liberals. Does a liberal have to deny that personal relationships involving love and intimacy are important to what or who we are?

It is my view that what the communitarian or care ethicist wants or needs to say against liberalism is better put in different, or at least more elaborate, terms. I think most liberals would claim that love relationships (not to mention community commitments) are important to us, and that such a view is entirely consistent with their moral and political views. But in what follows, I hope to show that liberals don't *entirely* have the right to say such things. Why this is so is far from obvious. So let me proceed, and I think the best way to begin is to introduce another argument or consideration that has sometimes been launched against Kant (or Kantians) in particular.

Thus it could be said that Kant doesn't merely treat love between individuals as unimportant, but advocates moral attitudes and dispositions that undercut the *possibility* both of love between individuals, and of strong personal commitment to ethnic, religious, and other communities. For example (to borrow from Bernard Williams), if an individual who is invariably conscientious in the way Kant most approves and admires is faced with a choice between saving his wife from drowning and saving some stranger, that individual will consult morality and determine that his moral views allow, or require, him to save his wife, before he actually goes in and tries to save her.[29] According to Williams, such a husband has 'one thought too many', and certainly his wife, were she ever to find out how he decided to save her, would have reason to complain about his love for her, reason to question whether he loved her as much as most spouses would like to be loved. But even if we grant this point, it doesn't follow that the man in Williams's example doesn't love his wife (and Williams never says that he doesn't); so the Kantian can claim – in the face of this and similar arguments – that no reason has been given to think that Kant's view of ideal morality undercuts the very possibility of love for individuals or of commitment to larger communities.[30]

Still, Kant may have a real problem if his ideal moral individual isn't capable of the *fullest sort* of love, and I want to argue now that not only Kant, but also contemporary liberals, have difficulty accommodating, or making sense of the value of, fully loving relationships. And like Williams's famous example of the husband saving his wife, my argument will attempt to demonstrate that liberal ideals of the person involve an individual, a person, who has (at least) 'one thought too many'.

Liberals subscribe to an ideal of personal autonomy that is somewhat different from anything mentioned so far in these pages. We have spoken of autonomy as involving a freedom to act without certain sorts of external interference, and of a right individuals may have to be free of various forms of such interference. We have also spoken of a (causally and/or constitutively relational) autonomy that involves an individual's deciding things and thinking for her- or himself. But this latter idea can be, and sometimes is, extended into a further ideal, the ideal of an individual willing and able to subject each and every one of her attachments, commitments, beliefs, and projects to critical scrutiny. This goes beyond the autonomy that is constituted by thinking and deciding for oneself, because it involves more self-consciousness and self-reflection than the latter requires. And also because it entails that one will later (occasionally) reconsider decisions and beliefs one has settled on earlier. Still, this ideal of *critical* autonomy is, in a sense, continuous with the idea of thinking and deciding for oneself. If one is willing and able to subject every-thing one thinks and wants to critical scrutiny, it is all the less likely (if it is possible at all) that one is under the sway of another's thinking or decision-making, or that one is being influenced by (either external or internal) causal factors that subvert or circumvent one's own capacity to think and choose. We can illustrate the notion of critical autonomy just introduced by reference to an issue that particularly concerns feminists.

Women are sometimes taken advantage of because they love their husbands or families too much, and are consequently unwilling or unable to assert their own prerogatives or needs. This obviously relates to the issues about patriarchy and female self-abnegation or selflessness that we discussed in Chapter 4, but, more importantly for our purposes at the moment, some liberals think that autonomy conceived as the exercise of a capacity to subject all one's desires, attachments, beliefs, and projects to self-conscious critical scrutiny constitutes a much-needed *safeguard against* the specific injustices and/or oppression that arise from a woman's being overly devoted or committed to either men or her family. (Obviously, men can be overly devoted too, and critical autonomy can also be of use to them.)

According to Martha Nussbaum, for example, '[t]he liberal tradition holds that emotions should not be trusted as guides to life without being sub-jected to some sort of critical scrutiny' and 'urg[es] people to ask whether their emotions are appropriate'.[31] Such critical scrutiny, such questioning, would help women avoid or end some of the injustices and oppression that follow on excesses of emotional commitment; and Nussbaum goes on to criticize Nel Noddings's views on caring for recommending emotional attitudes that are not sufficiently self-critical, and for regarding the critical attitude recommended by liberalism as involving 'one thought too many'. She then concludes by claim-ing that love and deep caring are '[f]ine, so long as you think first'.[32] Who is right here?

Well, consider a woman who loves her family – her parents, husband, and children – without ever having engaged with the question whether it is appropriate for her to love them or, say, with the question whether such feeling and/or the relationships she is involved in are a good thing for her. According to Nussbaum, she *should* raise these questions, and presumably should have done so earlier. But it does seem odd or ridiculous, doesn't it, for a woman to be questioning, say, her love for her parents without having any particular reason for being suspicious of that love?

However, if the woman lives in circumstances that can be described as (to some extent) patriarchal, then there is reason for her to wonder at least about her love for her husband. Perhaps he has taken unjust advantage of her devotion to him, and if she has hitherto been blind to this fact, perhaps it is time for her to wake up. Furthermore, patriarchal values have very possibly also influenced the way her father and mother have treated her, and presumably, then, she needs to take a critical look at her relationship with and feelings about them. And there may be similar reasons to look critically at her feelings about her children.

But Nussbaum makes it sound as if critical scrutiny is relevant to every aspect of one's feelings, and this means that the woman should at some point ask herself whether she should love her parents at all, whether she should (continue to) be involved in that kind of relationship with them, and this seems questionable even in circumstances of patriarchy. Even if patriarchy distorts and creates injustices in family relationships, that doesn't seem an adequate reason to question whether one should love one's parents. And the same point can be made even more forcefully with respect to one's feelings about one's children. The question 'Should I really love them' seems frighteningly out of place, even where there is a need to reconfigure or rework one's relationship with them. Of course, love for one's husband seems, and is, much less inevitable than these other feelings/relationships, and so, given patriarchal conditions, it *does* seem appropriate to consider (not every day, but at least at some time or other) whether that love, taken as a whole, is appropriate or advisable for one. But the point is that Nussbaum and other liberals don't make this distinction. They hold that every emotion or feeling should at some time or times be called into question, and even in patriarchal or other distorting, unjust circumstances, this doesn't seem to be true of all feelings or all relationships. The liberal is urging many thoughts too many.

Moreover, the liberal urges critical scrutiny of one's emotions/feelings in all circumstances, not just under conditions of patriarchy, and this claim too seems overly broad. Under patriarchy, there are reasons to be suspicious of what is happening in various relationships, danger signals that are really out there but that many women miss, downplay, or reinterpret because their autonomous thinking has to some extent been undermined. If a husband takes unfair advantage of his wife's selfless devotion, then it may well be appropriate for her to call the whole relationship, and her love for him, into question, and if she does not, then perhaps some consciousness-raising is called for. But if the circumstances aren't patriarchal and consciousness doesn't need raising, it doesn't seem appropriate for the woman to question her relationship with her husband and her other relationships. The liberal tells us that it is always appropriate to scrutinize our feelings and relationships, that we should maintain a kind of *critical vigilance*, regardless of circumstances. However, such an attitude in effect attenuates the feelings, the love, that one has toward others. If, independently of danger signals, we seriously ask whether we should love our children, our parents, or our spouses as much as we do, then in effect we don't love them as much as we could and as much as, ideally, we should. So by recommending critical vigilance, I think the liberal shows an insufficient appreciation of the value of love. If patriarchal circumstances make such vigilance necessary and advisable, then some of the value love can have for us or in our lives is (tragically) lost as a result, and the liberal just doesn't see this.[33]

Where critical vigilance *isn't* necessary, it in effect, then, involves at least one thought too many because it precludes the fullest and most ideal kind of love. Thus, in the example Williams mentioned, the wife would be aghast at learning that her husband had consulted moral rules or standards before deciding to save her rather than a stranger and would in particular see this as showing, or tending to show, that her husband loved her less than she had supposed or hoped. That is because we see love – at least the kind of love we aspire to and value deeply – as inconsistent with the kind of thinking done by the husband in Williams's example.[34]

Something similar can be said about a woman (or man) who thinks critically about whether the love they feel for, say, their parents is appropriate or a good thing for them. To seriously question one's attachment to or involvement with others in this way shows a certain fearfulness and distance that are incompatible with the fullest or best love, and where fear and distancing aren't called for, the questioning clearly seems to involve (a tendency toward) too many thoughts.

This doesn't mean that one shouldn't critically reconsider (or consider) one's love for somebody if one gets warning or danger signals that things are not as good or proceeding as well as they should be. But there is a difference between the actual critical thinking that is characteristic of critical vigilance and (merely) being disposed to think critically if things start to go or have gone wrong – what we can call *critical responsiveness*. And I want to say that where things are initially all right or better than all right, it is critical responsiveness that makes the most sense. In such circumstances, it is critical responsiveness, rather than critical vigilance, that allows the fullest and best kind of love to remain a possibility, and that is why the completely general attitude of critical vigilance or alertness recommended by Nussbaum seems not to be a good idea.[35]

Now Nussbaum is only one among many liberals who recommend that critical scrutiny precede, or at least accompany, emotional attachments. In *The Theory and Practice of Autonomy*, for example, Gerald Dworkin regards the critical scrutiny of one's (first-order) desires, commitments, and beliefs during the course of one's daily life as an ideal of autonomy that is generally to be recommended and emulated.[36] But he also engages the worry that such autonomy might be inconsistent with loyalty (or love), and claims that it is not. Dworkin may be right that there is no inconsistency between love and his ideal of autonomy, but if what I am saying is correct, then the kind of critical autonomy liberals like Dworkin and Nussbaum recommend *is* inconsistent with the fullest sort of love, with the sort of love most of us think is best and ourselves aspire to. So anyone who recommends such a critical attitude seems to undervalue love, even if they place some value on love and seek to accommodate love to, or reconcile it with, what they recommend.

The same point holds, basically, for Kant's ideal of thoroughgoing conscientiousness; so those who we saw earlier criticizing Kant for not accommodating love may be literally incorrect in what they say, but at least they seem to be on the right track. More strongly, those who criticize the liberal for treating relationships as inessential, in the sense of *unimportant*, to our identities turn out to have at least some *inkling* of what can (if the present argument is correct) be more accurately said against liberal views. Furthermore, the view of critical autonomy expressed by both Nussbaum and Dworkin, the view that it is, in general, good to take a critical attitude toward one's own beliefs, affections, commitments, and aspirations, is absolutely typical of liberal moral and political thinking, so if such a general attitude is suspect or worse, we have reason to question at least one important aspect of the liberal position. The liberal's unqualified approval of critical autonomy, the liberal's defense of what I am calling critical vigilance, represents or constitutes a devaluing, an insufficient appreciation of the value, of love (and other emotional commitments and dispositions, including attitudes of caring or concern about others – a point we shall return to in Chapter 7).

In Chapter 4, I said that autonomy, understood as the developed capacity for thinking for oneself and acting on one's own initiative, is something desirable that good/respectful parenting tends to produce. But the universal critical vigilance that liberals recommend seems, in the light of what we have just been saying, to be a distorted or exaggerated version of such autonomy, and I am certainly not recommending it. Moreover, to the extent that the liberal thinker devalues or undervalues love and strong emotional attachments more generally, s/he essentially underestimates the value and importance of *connection with other people*. And by the same token, what the liberal recommends in the way of critical distance from feelings or emotions toward others constitutes an overvaluation of separateness from others and of autonomy understood in at least one traditional way.

In that case, there may be reason to suspect what liberalism says about hate speech. The liberal thinks that freedom of speech, even of hate speech, shouldn't be interfered with, even in order to prevent substantial pain and even harm to others.[37] This places a certain value on separateness both from those who might want to interfere with one's free (hate) speech, and from those one's (hate) speech is likely to damage. By contrast, the care ethicist who thinks free speech should be interfered with in such cases places a (greater) value on our connection to, and responsibility for, other people. We already saw, however, that the liberal's preference for critical vigilance toward our feelings represents an underestimation of the value of connection with other people, and that gives us at least some reason to think that the liberal may place too little value on connection in cases involving freedom of speech, and so be overestimating our rights of autonomy against others in such cases. Alternatively, one could claim that the fact that the care ethicist emphasizes connection in the right way in regard to critical attitudes toward the emotions is some reason to think that what s/he says about connection with others in cases of hate speech is also correct.

Either way, one has an argument from or by analogy here, one with limited but real force. So if we buy the care-ethical critique of the liberal's preference for critical vigilance *vis-à-vis* the emotions, we have at least some reason to think that the care-ethical view of hate speech is preferable to that of the liberal. And if there is reason to think that care ethics is correct in an important range of cases where its moral judgments differ from those of the liberal or Kantian, doesn't that support care ethics against liberalism and Kantianism more generally? That more general support would be undercut or overridden, perhaps, if care ethics couldn't deliver the major forms of deontology that liberalism and common sense both accept. Or if the care ethicist had nothing substantial, interesting, and intuitive to say about autonomy. But I don't think care ethics is at all in that position, and in the light of what we have been arguing in the past two chapters, we may in fact want to say specifically that the liberal makes *too much* of autonomy. I believe that the more restricted ideals of autonomy, and of respect for autonomy, that care ethics can articulate and defend represent a more ethically adequate picture of what autonomy is all about than anything we find in the mainstream tradition of liberal moral and political philosophy. The disagreement between liberalism and care ethics doesn't seem to correlate very well with gender, but that doesn't in any way prevent the ethics of care from giving a better account than liberalism does of the morality of hate speech and of moral issues more generally. And so the importance and validity of care ethics simply don't depend on assumptions about gender differences.[38]

Now care ethics not only has a distinctive way of understanding autonomy, but also has its own non-traditional way(s) of understanding justice, and we shall discuss what an ethics of empathic caring can say about social and legal justice in the next chapter. But now we need to consider one further worry about what has just been said about the advantage care ethics has over liberalism and Kantianism. That advantage springs from what I have claimed to be a better account of the ethics of free speech, and what I tentatively concluded was that the care ethicist and/or feminist is right to advocate legal and personal interference with hate speech (remember the case of the daughter whose father is a neo-Nazi). I would like now, however, to mention some reasons why one should perhaps hesitate to advocate this particular solution to the problem of hate speech.

It is difficult to define 'hate speech', and not all forms of such speech are equally offensive and/or harmful. So if we think that the march in Skokie should have been banned and advocate legislation that would ban that kind of march, we have to worry about how that legislation should be framed and at

81

what level (federal, state, or local) it should take place. In the USA we will also need to consider how laws or ordinances against hate speech fit in with requirements of the Constitution, though amendments to the Constitution need not be totally out of the picture. These questions also raise issues about adjudication, about how easily or definitively judges will be able to interpret and resolve issues involving any given law or local ordinance or constitutional requirement.

Now someone who advocates a ban on hate speech in Skokie-type cases will presumably wish to do so, at least in part, because of the profound harm such speech is likely to cause.[39] One then needs to say how such cases differ from those in which speech that may give offense, and even to some extent cause harm, *should not be banned*. Also, if we wish to ban neo-Nazi hate speech in certain kinds of circumstances, we presumably will also want to ban similar kinds of speech, say, against blacks, but to do so in such a way that we will not thereby be prohibiting civil rights marches in places where there is a great deal of anti-black prejudice and hatred. It seems plausible to suppose that such a thing is in principle do-able: for example, civil rights marches may offend, frustrate, and enrage those prejudiced against blacks, but such marches don't humiliate, traumatize, and psychologically undermine prejudiced people in the way hate speech can affect blacks or Holocaust survivors.[40] And so to that extent, care ethicists who advocate limiting freedom of speech may be able, in defensible terms, to draw the line between speech they want to prohibit and speech they think should be allowed.[41] Even if different care ethicists might initially want to draw the line in different places, there is no reason to think those differences couldn't be discussed and possibly resolved in terms congenial to the ethics of caring (and, conceivably, with the help of newly discovered facts relevant to the discussion – remember how studies of the effect of segregation on blacks made a difference in *Brown versus Board of Education*).[42] But there is a further point that needs to be stressed.

The application of legislation to or in particular cases depends on the decision-making of judges (also of police officers and of various governmental officials, but let me simplify), and most of us are familiar with some of the historic and present-day difficulties of legal adjudication. But the application of laws banning hate speech makes special demands that don't arise in many other kinds of adjudication, and that fact is worth considering, A judge who has to decide whether certain speech falls under a ban on speech intended to humiliate and/or wound members of a certain race, ethnicity, religion, or gender, has to be able to think cogently and sensitively about people's intentions, has to be able to tell the difference, for example, between malign intentions and intentions that inadvertently wound others.[43] But the victims of hate speech are also sensitive to this latter difference, and part of the harm they suffer comes from their recognition of the difference between someone trying to wound them and someone doing so inadvertently. A judge needs to be able to understand facts like this if s/he is to make good decisions in 'hard cases', and such understanding requires a certain degree of empathy that may not be (as) necessary in other kinds of adjudication.[44]

It is perhaps even more obvious that legislators considering laws banning certain forms of hate speech will need to be empathically sensitive if they are to pass good laws. In the next chapter, I argue that good or just legislation can, in general, be conceived in terms of appropriately empathic concern for others on the part of legislators, but my worry at the moment is that, in present-day circumstances, we can't assume that legislators *are* (sufficiently) empathic. Nor can we assume that even empathic legislators will be immune to political pressures that give them self-interested reasons not to consider, or at least not to pass, laws banning hate speech. So if the care ethicist advocates legislation banning hate speech, s/he has to realize that there may be considerable practical difficulties in bringing about such legislation.

A similar point about political pressures also applies to judges, and these problems, taken together, raise a further issue that care ethicists need to consider. If defensible hate speech legislation is passed, it is possible, because of political pressures, for judges to misinterpret or misapply it. And it is also possible for politically motivated legislators to pass laws that ban other sorts of speech we would like to permit and even encourage. As my friend Scott Gelfand has suggested (to me), religious lobbyists might well put pressure on legislatures to ban speech questioning the divinity of Christ, or, as Feinberg puts it, 'if the swastika and burning crosses are banned today on good grounds, relatively innocuous symbols may be banned tomorrow on not so good grounds'.[45] So anyone who advocates legislation banning certain sorts of hate speech should realize that what they are advocating may be perverted, distorted, or overextended by others, and these facts might well make a difference to what care ethicists or some feminists want to say about these issues.

But none of this constitutes a challenge to the plausibility or legitimacy of care ethics. In the first place, both liberals and care ethicists have some tendency to think about the question of banning hate speech in relative isolation from considerations having to do with the potential corruption of legal and judicial processes. The typical liberal bases his or her defense of hate speech on considerations of autonomy, rather than on the potential 'slippery slope' effects of banning such speech. And by the same token, the care ethicist can, in effect, be seen as saying that if we don't worry about the political ill effects of passing laws against hate speech, there are moral reasons to pass such laws, as saying, in other words, that such laws are legitimate *apart from or in the absence of* slippery slope considerations. Liberalism seems to disagree with care ethics on precisely this point, and the analysis above seeks not only to explain the disagreement, but to defend one side of it. The potential for political corruption doesn't, therefore, undercut the main points made earlier, but it is also worth considering whether the ethics of care can say something morally relevant to the issue of corruption. I think it can.

If legislation banning certain forms of hate speech can be abused or misused by legislators or judges, then a thoroughgoing ethics of care needs to say something about such scenarios. It is one thing to say, and have good moral reason to say, that hate speech should be banned in circumstances where we don't need to worry about political, slippery slope considerations, but we may want to say something different about circumstances where there is a real danger, for example, that political forces will use hate-speech legislation as a pretext for banning speech that care ethicists and others would want to see protected. I think the care ethicist at least ought to concede this point, but argue that if there are political, slippery slope reasons for hesitating or refusing to ban hate speech, those reasons can be unpacked in terms congenial to care ethics.[46] So I believe there is no reason in principle why a care ethicist couldn't or shouldn't hesitate or refuse to advocate legislation against hate speech in circumstances where such a ban was likely to lead to undesirable and harmful bans on other sorts of speech. But, as I have said, the deepest disagreement between care ethicists and liberals centers around the notion of autonomy, and we have been given some reason to think that care ethics has the better of *that* argument.

3. Paternalism

We have so far been discussing cases where there is a question of whether someone should intervene to prevent someone else from harming third parties, and we have seen a crucial disagreement between liberalism and care ethics concerning certain cases of this sort. But there are also situations where someone has to decide whether to intervene to prevent a person from harming him- or herself, situations that fall under the familiar rubric of paternalism, and I have avoided discussing that kind of case until now (at least in the present chapter). My main reason has been that it is less clear that care ethics will or should want to disagree with liberalism about paternalistic examples. This needs some explaining.

Liberals are generally wary of paternalism, and the value they place on autonomy lies behind that wariness. For just as (traditionally conceived) autonomy considerations may seem to justify a refusal to interfere with individual liberties for the sake of preventing harm to third parties, they can just as easily seem to justify a refusal to interfere with someone's liberty to do or risk harm (solely) to herself. Of course, there are circumstances in which even liberals think such paternalistic intervention is justified – for example when minor children are involved. And there is also some disagreement among them about the (other) kinds of considerations or circumstances that can make paternalistic intervention permissible or even obligatory.[47] But none of this is any surprise. What *might* surprise, however, is the fact that the care ethicist might also be suspicious of paternalism, though on grounds very different from those that influence the liberal. Care ethics may wish to base an objection to paternalism on considerations having to do with (the value of) our connection with others, rather than, as the liberal would have it, on (the value of) our autonomy or separateness from others; and we need to see how a common opposition to (most forms of) paternalism can be generated from such different, such *opposed*, reasons.

Now empathy connects us with others in a desirable way, and empathy has certainly been at the heart of our account, until now, of individual and political morality. But you can't derive opposition to paternalism from considerations of empathy alone. For just as a parent who takes his unwilling child to the doctor's may not be lacking in empathy for that child, I believe it is possible to empathize completely with those who want to ride a motorcycle with their hair blowing freely in the wind and yet insist that such people wear a helmet for their own good. If (some) care ethicists wish to oppose most forms of paternalism, they will need to invoke other considerations.

Care ethics is typically regarded as an ethics of relationships more than of individual obligations and virtues. There may, for example, be something less than ideal, and to that extent ethically unsatisfactory, about a mother–child relationship in which the child in no way acknowledges the mother's caring – though, as I mentioned earlier, such acknowledgement doesn't have to involve (an explicit expression of) gratitude and might simply take the form of contented cooing and smiling. And for similar reasons, an ethic of care may want to say that there is something ethically unsatisfactory in making motorcyclists wear a helmet. If the cyclist, given his or her values, would never positively acknowledge or accept an intervention that prevented him from (or coerced him into not) riding without a helmet, if the cyclist resents such intervention as a violation of his or her fundamental values, then such intervention might properly be regarded as inconsistent with good relationship, even if it is based in, or consistent with, empathic understanding of or concern with 'where the motorcyclist is coming from' on the part of the person who intervenes. This would still allow a parent to take an unwilling child to the doctor's, because it can be reasonably assumed that, as an adult, the child will or would someday acknowledge and accept the caring aspect of what the parent had coercively done earlier. But in the case of the motorcyclist, we are assuming that the intervener has no reason to think the cyclist will ever accept what s/he has done (even if it prevents death or greater injury in the case of an accident); and so an ethics of care that emphasizes good relationships as a basis for evaluating individual actions can say that paternalistic interventions that will never and would never be acknowledged are morally forbidden.[48]

This takes us beyond issues of empathy, and if we move in this direction, our earlier account of respect (for autonomy) needs to be supplemented by the further consideration just mentioned. But I am not entirely sure care ethics *should* go in this direction. Is it so clear that an empathic, caring person, having exhausted the possibilities of persuasion, wouldn't try to prevent someone – for example their own grown-up child or some other person they love – from riding a motorcycle without a helmet? And wouldn't the unflinchingly paternalistic, but completely empathic concern of the intervener possibly outweigh, or at least counterbalance, the cyclist's resentment when it came to assessing the value of their relationship? I'm not sure, and it seems to me, therefore, that care ethics needs to think a great deal more before it settles for a definitive answer to questions about paternalism. The care ethicist may, in the end, want to agree with the liberal about the general moral undesirability of paternalistic interventions – while basing that agreement on the value of connection rather than the diametrically opposed considerations of autonomy that the liberal invokes. But if the care ethicist moves in this direction, s/he will have to interpret the value of connection in a very particular way – as depending on potential acceptance of caring on the part of one cared for. (This interpretation would be very much in keeping with some of the things Nel Noddings says about the value of connection/relationships.)

On the other hand, we saw above that a care ethicist might ultimately *disagree* with the liberal about the permissibility of paternalistic interventions, and if that happened, it would be because, in the end, the care ethicist regarded empathic caring as embodying as much connection to others as it is *morally* desirable for an individual to have. Something like this idea can be found in Gilligan's writings, and if one accepts it, then the general correlation between moral distinctions and distinctions of empathy we have so far uncovered in a variety of instances will also be exemplified in cases where issues of paternalism arise.[49] From the standpoint of the present book, that is a reason to resist assuming that the value care ethics places on connection forces it into ironic agreement with the general opposition to paternalism that liberalism defends in terms of the value of separateness. For the argument and conclusions of this book depend on there being a pretty general correlation between facts about empathy and facts or intuitions about morality, and the more general the better. But, because of complications in the area of paternalism, it just isn't clear at this point that the correlation is perfect and that our conclusions, therefore, will be as thoroughly supported as one (or I) might like.

I should add that the discussion here, and this whole general argument, are also neutral on a further question that we haven't spoken of since much earlier in this book. Many care ethicists object to virtue ethics on the grounds that it sees moral value as residing primarily in individuals or individual traits or motives, rather than in relationships, and in my own previous work I have argued that the individual trait or virtue of (empathic) caring is ethically more fundamental than caring relationships.[50] But until we are in a position to say more about the issues we have just been discussing, I think we should not try to decide which aspect or kind of caring is ethically primary or fundamental (or whether either is).

Finally, it needs to be noted that, even if we were to grant acknowledgement and acceptance a crucial ethical role, that wouldn't substantially affect the argument for banning hate speech offered earlier. When you deny someone the right to speak in certain ways, you may well be intervening in a way they would never accept, but if we give permission to hate speech out of a consideration of that very fact, then we act *toward other people* in ways that *they* would never accept. For example, we permit neo-Nazis to speak or demonstrate near the homes of Holocaust survivors, and this is something the survivors are never likely to find acceptable. In such cases, we have to weigh one person's non-acceptance against another's, and either our relationship with the neo-Nazis or our relationship with the Holocaust survivors may turn out to be characterized by ethically undesirable non-acceptance or non-acknowledgement. In the presence of such conflict, any ethics of care needs to make a decision, and there is no reason why that decision cannot be based on the other factors an ethics of care takes into account. Yes, an interference with the neo-Nazis' freedom to march and speak is frustrating to them, but the harm, if any, that entails is arguably insignificant by comparison with the harm that would likely be suffered by the Holocaust survivors if the march were allowed. An empathic concern for people that is sensitive to all the factors in Skokie-type cases can hold it to be wrong to allow such a march to go forward, and also wrong (or morally less desirable) for the woman in our earlier example to do nothing to prevent her father from attending such a march.

In pure cases of paternalism, on the other hand, there can be a univocal issue of acceptance/acknowledgement. If one allows a person to ride a motorcycle without a helmet, and the sole issue is the damage he may do to himself, then even if what one does is not in the person's best interests, there is or may be no-one who is unwilling to acknowledge or accept what one has done. Of course, most cases of paternalism are not pure – there are other parties whose welfare or interests are involved. For example, helmet laws – and seatbelt laws for drivers – are often justified by reference to the costs the public has to bear when a cyclist or driver has an accident. But then the justification for the legislation is no longer purely paternalistic, and an ethics of care that stressed acceptance probably also wouldn't want to rule out in advance the moral relevance of the effects of riding without a helmet or driving without a seatbelt on the welfare of *the family* of those who ride or drive in those ways. But in any event, the possibilities we have been considering in this section needn't, I think, undermine conclusions reached earlier in this chapter or in previous chapters as well.

We have spent time on political and legal issues in the present chapter and also, to some extent, in previous chapters. But I have not offered any considered general view about what social justice involves, and it is time now to develop our ethics of care in a more systematically political way.

Notes

1 See Susan Brison, 'The Autonomy Defense of Free Speech', *Ethics* 108, 1998, pp. 312–39, for copious references to – and trenchant criticisms of – the 'autonomy defenses' of free speech that have been offered by Dworkin, Nagel, Scanlon, and

many others. The present discussion can be seen as a response to this article *in the light* of the ethics of empathic care.

2 For objections to allowing various forms of hate speech, see e.g. Susan Brownmiller, *Against Our Will: Men, Women, and Rape*, New York: Simon & Schuster, 1975, esp. p. 395; Catharine MacKinnon, *Only Words*, Cambridge, MA: Harvard University Press, 1993, esp. pp. 82f., 105f.; Catharine MacKinnon, *Women's Lives – Men's Laws*, Cambridge, MA: Harvard University Press, 2005, esp. p. 64.; and several of the essays collected in L. Lederer and R. Delgado, eds, *The Price We Pay: The Case Against Racist Speech, Hate Propaganda, and Pornography*, New York: Hill & Wang, 1995. Both Brownmiller and MacKinnon, and several of the authors in the Lederer/ Delgado volume, focus largely on pornography, arguing that it is or can be a form of hate speech, and as such should be legally restricted or banned; but these authors also favor restricting or banning hate speech in the more ordinary understanding of the term.

3 Scanlon defends hate speech with explicit reference to Skokie (and relevant court decisions): Thomas Scanlon, 'Freedom of Expression and Categories of Expression', *University of Pittsburgh Law Review* 40, 1979, pp. 511–50. Catharine MacKinnon (*ibid.*) opposes hate speech with specific reference to Skokie.

4 But the toupee or teeth are the man's property, and the daughter is temporarily depriving him of the use of them. Isn't that a reason (for care ethics) to say that what she does isn't morally acceptable? Not necessarily. After all, almost everyone thinks it is all right to deprive someone temporarily of the use of their property, if that is necessary to the preservation of life and limb. For example, we think it permissible for someone temporarily to commandeer a person's jacuzzi if it is needed to help prevent some third party's wound from becoming gangrenous. The liberal may say that depriving someone of the use of property *isn't* morally justified when the sole purpose of doing so is to prevent them from giving vent to harmful hate speech; but the gangrene example should make it clear how and why a care ethicist might disagree. However, as Susan Brison has pointed out to me, hiding false teeth interferes with normal bodily functioning and may be morally questionable for that reason. The alternative example of hiding a toupee doesn't have this problem.

5 Nancy Chodorow, *The Reproduction of Mothering*, Berkeley, CA: University of California Press, 1978.

6 Here for simplicity's sake I am ignoring the qualifications about educational or socio-economic status, and about time and place, that Gilligan and others sometimes note and insist on (cf. Joan Tronto, *Moral Boundaries: A Political Argument for an Ethic of Care*, New York: Routledge, 1993, Ch. 3).

7 Nancy Chodorow, *The Reproduction of Mothering*, op. cit., pp. 87ff., 217ff. I am simplifying matters here by not speaking of the distinction between sex and gender, and by not considering the kinds of voices homosexuals, lesbians, transsexuals, and others might have.

8 Carol Gilligan, 'Moral Orientation and Moral Development' in E. Kittay and D. Meyers, eds, *Women and Moral Theory*, Totowa, NJ: Rowman & Littlefield, 1987, pp. 19–33.

9 However, Gilligan (*ibid.*) makes free use of Chodorow's work and gives no indication of thinking (as I am about to argue here) that the findings she reports call that work into question.

10 It has been said that we should be skeptical about the voice of caring (and any ethics based on it) because women's caring tendencies may very well result from their disadvantaged (or relatively helpless) position in society, and serve the interests of patriarchy (e.g. Catharine MacKinnon, *Feminism Unmodified*, Cambridge, MA: Harvard University Press, 1987, p.45; Claudia Card, 'Gender and Moral Luck'

in V. Held, ed., *Justice and Care: Essential Readings in Feminist Ethics*, Boulder, CO: Westview Press, 1995, pp. 79–98). We saw earlier that something like this is probably true of exaggerated, 'selfless' versions/instances of caring; but to say this about caring in general is to ignore the fact that many women think and make decisions in terms of justice rather than caring. Just as Chodorow's purported explanation of why men value separation and think in terms of justice cannot (without essential modification or qualification) account for the fact that so many women think in terms of justice, the claim that care thinking is an artifact of subordination also leaves us with no explanation of why so many (presumably subordinated) women think in terms of justice. I don't think this kind of criticism or skepticism gives us a reason to reject care ethics in advance of seeing how well such ethics can account for ethical phenomena.

11 For two examples, see the work of Martha Nussbaum (note 31) and Diana Meyers's 'Rights in Collision: A Non-punitive Compensatory Remedy for Abusive Speech', *Law and Philosophy* 14, 1995, pp. 203–43, where (the right to give public expression to) hate speech is defended by reference to considerations of autonomy. I should add that there are also many women who defend (permitting) hate speech on *libertarian* grounds: e.g. Camille Paglia, *Vamps and Tramps*, New York: Vintage Books, 1994, pp. 50f.

12 Nancy Chodorow, *The Reproduction of Mothering, op. cit., passim*; also Carol Gilligan, *In a Different Voice: Psychological Theory and Women's Development*, Cambridge, MA: Harvard University Press, 1982, pp. 7–8.

13 See e.g. Tania Singer *et al.*, 'Empathic Neural Responses are Modulated by the Perceived Fairness of Others', *Nature* 439, 2006, pp. 466–69; Tania Singer *et al.*, 'Empathy for Pain Involves the Affective but not Sensory Components of Pain', *Science* 303, 2004, pp. 1157–62; E. J. Hermans *et al.*, 'Testosterone Administration Reduces Empathetic Behavior: A Facial Mimicry Study', *Psychoneuroendocrinology* 31, 2006, pp. 859–66; S. Baron-Cohen, 'The Extreme Male Brain Theory of Autism', *Trends in Cognitive Science* 6, 2002, pp. 248–54; S. Baron-Cohen, *The Essential Difference: The Male and Female Brain, and the Riddle of Autism*, London: Penguin, 2003; R. Knickmeyer, S. Baron-Cohen, P. Raggatt, K. Taylor and G. Hackett, 'Fetal Testosterone and Empathy', *Hormones and Behavior* 49, 2006, pp. 282–92; J. A. Harris, J. P. Rushton, E. Hampson and D.N. Jackson, 'Salivary Testosterone and Self-Report Aggressive and Pro-Social Personality Characteristics in Men and Women', *Aggressive Behavior* 22, 1996, pp. 321–31; and, for a book that summarizes and popularizes recent findings, Louann Brizendine, *The Female Brain*, New York: Morgan Road Books, 2006.

14 See, for example, Carol Gilligan and Grant Wiggins, 'The Origins of Morality in Early Childhood Relationships', in Jerome Kagan and Sharon Lamb, eds, *The Emergence of Morality in Young Children*, Chicago, IL: University of Chicago Press, 1987, esp. p. 279.

15 Lawrence Blum, 'Care' in L. Becker and C. Becker, eds, *Encyclopedia of Ethics*, Volume I, New York: Garland Publishing, 1992, p. 126.

16 Immanuel Kant, *Observations on the Feeling of the Beautiful and Sublime*, Berkeley, CA: University of California Press, 1960, pp. 76–81.

17 Even if men are, at present, less empathic overall than women, there may be important respects in which they now tend to be more empathic. If contemporary women demonstrate more of a tendency toward substitute success syndrome than men do, then in that respect men would tend to be more empathic, or at least less unempathic, than women. Men and women might then show a disposition toward *opposite moral vices*, with more men more frequently being *too distant* from others to be able to empathize with them, and women more frequently being *too close* to others to be able to empathize with them.

18 Recent studies show that men are less willing than women to acknowledge having empathically derived feelings, but some researchers have speculated that this may say less about basic differences between men and women than about social norms regarding the appropriateness of men or women expressing (or recognizing) their empathy-based feelings. On these points, see Randy Lemon and Nancy Eisenberg's 'Gender and Age Differences in Empathy and Sympathy' and C. Daniel Batson, Jim Fultz and Patricia A. Schoenrade's 'Adults' Emotional Reactions to the Distress of Others', both in N. Eisenberg and J. Strayer, eds, *Empathy and its Development*, Cambridge: Cambridge University Press, 1990.

19 Nel Noddings has suggested that boys be encouraged/taught to take more care of younger children both at home and at school. See Nel Noddings, *Educating Moral People: A Caring Alternative to Character Education*, New York: Teachers College Press; 2002. This is just one way in which social attitudes and male empathic tendencies might be altered.

20 All but the first two works cited in note 13 are directly relevant to this issue. It is perhaps also worth noting that in 'Reply by Carol Gilligan' (*Signs* 11, 1986, pp. 331ff.), Gilligan briefly discusses the relevance of greater male aggressiveness to morality.

21 On the comparison between autism and maleness, see the works of S. Baron-Cohen and Louann Brizendine, *op. cit.* (note 13).

22 Compare Katha Pollitt's 'Are Women Morally Superior to Men?' (*The Nation*, December 28, 1992, pp. 799–807), where it is noted that the thesis of women's superiority naturally emerges from views like Gilligan's, and where it is pointed out that although women may find this thesis flattering, men may like it because it lets them morally off the hook. As I have argued above, however, these (in gender terms) rather balanced implications of Gilligan's views or of care ethics don't have a lot of force against the idea of female moral superiority.

23 We have argued that women may be morally superior to men because of their greater empathy. An alternative argument for female superiority that has sometimes been given refers to the fact that women tend to be politically to the left of men – what is nowadays called the 'gender gap'. (See e.g. C. P. McCue and J. D. Gopoian, 'Dispositional Empathy and the Political Gender Gap', *Women & Politics* 21, 2000, pp. 1–20.) This argument can be reinforced if one accepts a sentimentalist ethics of care. (The Archbishop of Recife, making a political point humorously, once said 'the heart is a little to the left'.) But I don't think it would be useful to engage further with (the complexities of) this line of thought here.

24 John Rawls, *A Theory of Justice*, Cambridge, MA: Harvard University Press, 1971, sections 5, 6, 30.

25 There is no sense in giving references to feminists and care ethicists who claim that liberalism has a falsely atomistic and non-relational view of persons. Most of the works by feminists and care ethicists cited here make this sort of claim explicitly. For a communitarian source of similar ideas, see note 27.

26 John Rawls, *A Theory of Justice*, *op. cit.*, pp. 560–63. However, in subsequent work (e.g. *Political Liberalism*), Rawls denies having, or ever having had, a genuinely metaphysical theory of the nature of selves. Rather, he regards what he says about selves in *A Theory of Justice* as an expository device for representing the reasoning that occurs behind the veil of ignorance.

27 Michael J. Sandel, *Liberalism and the Limits of Justice*, Cambridge: Cambridge University Press, 1982, esp. Ch. 1 and Conclusion.

28 Saul Kripke, *Naming and Necessity*, Oxford: Blackwell, 1980.

29 Bernard Williams, 'Persons, Character, and Morality' in *Moral Luck*, Cambridge: Cambridge University Press, 1981.

30 This is precisely what that the Kantian Thomas Hill (Jr) *does* claim in 'The Importance of Autonomy' in *Autonomy and Self-Respect*, Cambridge: Cambridge University Press, 1987.

31 Martha Nussbaum, *Sex and Social Justice*, New York: Oxford University Press, 1999, pp. 74ff.

32 Martha Nussbaum, *ibid.*, p. 79. As far as I am able to tell, Nel Noddings's *Caring: A Feminine Approach to Ethics and Moral Education* (Berkeley, CA: University of California Press, 1984) doesn't make explicit reference to Williams's view that certain attitudes involve 'one thought too many'. But in using this phrase, Nussbaum usefully highlights the/a sense in which caring ethicists like Noddings commend or idealize a critically unselfconscious form of love or caring. I shall be arguing here – very explicitly – that liberalism *does* commit us to one thought too many.

33 At one point in her discussion, Nussbaum says that (what I am calling) critical vigilance might not be necessary if society were perfect; but she almost immediately goes on to suggest that love subjected to criticism is the healthiest kind of love. This fails to recognize what is lost when (given that society isn't perfect) love is, and has to be, subjected to criticism. What is lost is some of the value love can have for us, and Nussbaum fails to see or appreciate that value. Which is another way of saying that she, like other liberals, devalues or undervalues love.

34 Others have made the same basic point. See e.g. Susan Mendus, 'Some Mistakes about Impartiality', *Political Studies* XLIV, 1996, p. 323.

35 As indicated above, women who under patriarchy doubt their own voice are likely to discount or reinterpret danger signals and clearly don't count as (even) critically responsive. In urging critical responsiveness, therefore, I am (once again) criticizing attitudes and circumstances that undermine women's capacity for helping themselves. All this will be related to themes of justice in Chapter 6, but my main point here is that the fact that patriarchy undermines critical responsiveness is no reason to urge women or others to be *more* than critically responsive under patriarchy or in any other circumstances. Under patriarchy, those who are critically responsive will be able to criticize what is happening to them and to work for changes in their lives and in society generally. And so I am recommending critical responsiveness rather than critical vigilance as a universally appropriate and valuable attitude.

36 Gerald Dworkin, *The Theory and Practice of Autonomy*, Cambridge: Cambridge University Press, 1988, esp. pp. 20ff.

37 As Susan Brison points out ('The Autonomy Defense of Free Speech', *op. cit.*), liberals also tend to underestimate and misconceive the nature of the harms that result from hate speech. They speak a great deal about the 'moral' losses attendant on forbidding free (hate) speech, and they often focus on whether those who hear or learn about permitted hate speech will be encouraged to inflict physical harm on a target group and think of the targets of such speech as not suffering any real damage through the speech itself. This is a 'sticks-and-stones' view of the harm, or lack of it, that speech can inflict, and it makes one, makes me at least, wonder whether liberals have been sufficiently empathic with what it would have been like, say, for Holocaust survivors to have had to hear (about) neo-Nazis in jackboots parading through their town. Such an experience would have been likely to be more than unpleasant and painful; it could easily, for many of the survivors and others, have been (re)traumatizing in a way that would leave them psychologically and psychosomatically (even more) damaged. The liberal's failure fully to appreciate the extent and depth of the damage inflicted by hate speech may really show an insufficiently developed capacity for empathy. For more on the way speech can harm, and not merely cause suffering, see Susan Brison, 'Speech, Harm, and the Mind-Body Problem in First Amendment Jurisprudence', *Legal Theory* 4, 1998, pp. 39–61.

38 Compare Carol Gilligan, who in *In a Different Voice* (*op. cit.*, p. 2) and elsewhere says that the significance of the distinction between care thinking and justice thinking is independent of its correlation with sex or gender.

39 Joel Feinberg usefully introduces the term 'Skokie-type cases' in *Offense to Others*, Volume 2 of *The Moral Limits of the Criminal Law*, New York: Oxford University Press, 1985, pp. 86–96. Though Feinberg thinks the march should have been allowed, given the actual facts of the case, he also considers conceivable variations on the actual facts that he thinks would have justified a ban. However, I think Feinberg's discussion seriously underestimates the harms to Holocaust survivors that would or could have occurred if the march had taken place.

40 Also, a lesser degree of concern for frustration and offense felt as a result of thwarted hatred and prejudice, rather than thwarted neutral or positive feelings, may be consistent with an ethics of empathic caring and attributable to empathy itself. Martin Hoffman describes how empathy can lead one to feel angry with those who hurt and hate others, but this is a large topic best left to another occasion.

41 My focus here, and in what follows, is on what care ethics can say in response to 'slippery slope' and related arguments: hence the emphasis on different levels of hurt or harm and how empathy would respond to these. But feminists such as Catharine MacKinnon reject the ethics of care and focus on the discriminatory aspects of hate speech (while not downplaying the harm hate speech does). This different emphasis calls for a somewhat different response to slippery slope arguments from that developed in the text above. But my main purpose is to consider how the ethics of care can deal with various difficulties. For a response to MacKinnon's critique of care ethics, see note 10.

42 In particular, a credible care ethics needs to be able to show that legislation banning speech that merely offends, or that doesn't cause harm to the extent hate speech (sometimes or often) does, is inconsistent with relevant empathic concern. I assume this can be done if one can claim that such legislation would work against the welfare of human beings in society to a greater extent than allowing offensive or relatively harmless speech. And this is precisely what care ethics seems plausibly to be able to *deny* in the case of (the worst kinds of) hate speech. (As we shall see in Chapter 6, all these issues can be framed in terms of justice.)

43 But one has to be very careful in drawing this distinction because seemingly inadvertent remarks can sometimes reveal subconscious prejudice or malice – as, for example, most of us assume was the case with Mel Gibson's recent anti-Semitic comments made while under the influence.

44 For interesting discussion of the empathic sensitivities judges need in applying the law or the Constitution to the circumstances of particular cases, see Martha Nussbaum's 'Poets and Judges' in *Poetic Justice: The Literary Imagination and Public Life*, Boston, MA: Beacon Press, 1995, pp. 79–121. However, Ellen Frankel Paul has pointed out to me that there is a certain danger in encouraging judges to feel empathy in cases where, for example, there is an issue of limiting civil liberties: a judge might overestimate the damage neo-Nazi hate speech might cause out of a blind hatred for neo-Nazis that was *masquerading* as empathy for their potential victims. Of course, all legal systems are subject to abuse, but the care-ethical account of morality and justice arguably yields distinctive possibilities of abuse. However, even if this is so, it is worth noting that *any* distinctive theory of morality is likely to yield distinct ways in which morality can be violated *or* abused. Furthermore, judges take an oath to uphold the law, and given our empathy-involving account of the obligation to keep promises, there is reason to think that empathy can (also) act as a constraint on what they might do out of either hatred toward neo-Nazis or empathic concern for those who might be hurt or damaged by neo-Nazi hate speech. And it

can presumably also act as a (deontological) constraint on what judges and other public officials do in other cases, as well. Finally, there are parallel (and further) issues concerning the advisability of empathic feelings in doctors and nurses that I propose to take up in a separate context. However, for an eloquent and persuasive account of why empathy doesn't undercut medical professionalism and is actually *helpful* in doctor–patient relationships, see Jodi Halpern, *From Detached Concern to Empathy*, New York: Oxford University Press, 2001.

45 Joel Feinberg, *Offense to Others*, *op. cit.*, p. 93. My discussion here has been influenced by what Feinberg has to say about similar issues.

46 In speaking here of the reasons available to care ethics, I don't mean to suggest that care ethics seeks to show that moral claims are requirements of rationality, or are based in reason rather than sentiment. The reasons a moral view offers for its conclusions may simply be the considerations that it finds relevant to moral conclusions, but this leaves open the question whether moral requirements are requirements of practical rationality, and the question whether morality is based on pure reason. I will be discussing these further issues in Chapter 7.

47 For relevant discussion, see e.g. Joel Feinberg, *Harm to Self*, Volume 3 of *The Moral Limits of the Criminal Law*, New York: Oxford University Press, 1986; Robert Young, *Personal Autonomy: Beyond Negative and Positive Liberty*, New York: St Martin's Press, 1986.

48 I am speaking here vaguely of conditions under which interventions would be accepted or acknowledged, and more eventually needs to be said about what *kinds* of merely potential acknowledgement are consistent with good caring relationships and morally acceptable treatment of others.

49 Carol Gilligan ('Moral Orientation and Moral Development', *op. cit.*) says that the caring 'voice' reverses the traditional moral pattern of figure and ground: it views relationship(s) rather than individuals as figure, and individual identity rather than relationship(s) as secondary or in the background. And she also seems to regard an ethics that emphasizes responsiveness to others (rather than individual rights of autonomy against others) as treating connection and/or relationship as moral figure. In that case, a person who is empathically responsive to another might intervene paternalistically without displaying a lesser degree of (the value or importance of) connection. (Also compare what Gilligan says about connection with others: Carol Gilligan, 'Hearing the Difference: Theorizing Connection', *Anuario de Psicologia* 34, 2003, p. 156.)

50 For examples of care ethicists who insist on the primacy of relationships, see Virginia Held, 'The Ethics of Care' in David Copp, ed., *The Oxford Handbook of Ethical Theory*, New York: Oxford University Press, 2006, p. 551; Nel Noddings, 'Caring as Relation and Virtue in Teaching' in Rebecca L. Walker and Philip J. Ivanhoe, eds, *Working Virtue: Virtue Ethics and Contemporary Moral Problems*, New York: Oxford University Press, 2007, pp. 41–60. For my own opposed view see Michael Slote, *Morals from Motives*, New York: Oxford University Press, 2001, Ch. 1. But it is also worth noting the possibility that caring as a virtue and caring as a form of relationship are *equally* fundamental – that neither derives its ethical value from the other. This view, too, would be consistent with what I am saying here.

6

SOCIAL JUSTICE

1. The Empathy in Justice

In Chapter 4, I attempted to explain respect for autonomy in terms of an ethics of care, and I propose now to do the same kind of thing with regard to social justice. I have made substantial efforts in this direction in previous work, but this will be the first time that I shall be incorporating considerations having to do with empathy into a theory, or view, of what justice involves. (I shall not have much to say about rights because a theory of rights can be given in a fairly unproblematic way once a theory of justice has been accepted.)

I think it is possible to understand the justice of laws, institutions, and social customs *on analogy with* the ethics of individual (acts and attitudes of) caring. The ethics of empathic caring evaluates the actions of individuals in terms of whether they express, exhibit, or reflect empathically caring motivation, or its opposite, on the part of individuals.[1] But the laws, institutions, and customs of a given society are like the actions of that society, for they reflect or express the motives (and beliefs) of the social group (or sub-groups) in something like the way that individual actions reflect or express an agent's motives (and beliefs), though in a more enduring manner that seems appropriate to the way societies typically outlast the individual agents in them. So an ethics of empathic caring can say that institutions and laws, as well as social customs and practices, are just if they reflect empathically caring motivation on the part of (enough of) those responsible for originating and maintaining them. But let me be a bit more specific.

We saw earlier that people are likely to develop more empathy for (groups of) people they know than for those they don't. Still, and as I mentioned, we do have the capacity to develop *some* substantial empathy and concern for distant people we don't know, and in that case it is perhaps not too much to expect people to develop a *greater degree* of empathic concern *for their compatriots*. We tend to have a lot more in common with compatriots or fellow citizens than with most of the inhabitants of other countries, and even if we don't know, aren't personally acquainted with, many of the citizens of our country, we are part of, and therefore well acquainted with, the national group, the nation, of which they are all members – and with its common or general culture.

So let us consider the national legislators who originate or pass a given law. And let us simplify matters by assuming it is only their motivation toward fellow citizens that is relevant to the assessment of the legislation they pass.[2] In that case, we can say, to begin with, that a law is just if it reflects or expresses empathically caring motivation toward their compatriots on the part of the legislative group that is responsible for passing it.[3] But, less demandingly, an ethic of empathic care will also want to say that a law is just even if it merely fails to reflect or exhibit a *lack* of appropriate empathic concern on the part of those who promulgate it. Not every action of a malicious person necessarily reflects that maliciousness, and when a malicious person scratches his head, for example, we can say that that action is morally all right because it in no way expresses or reflects that person's malice. And by the same token, morally unsavory national legislators who were largely indifferent to the welfare of their compatriots, to the good of their country, might pass a law that in no way displayed or reflected their greediness or selfishness: for example, a law allowing right turns at stoplights throughout the nation. That law would be just, or at least not unjust, according to the view I am now defending.[4] We now need to see whether we arrive at plausible judgments about what is or is not just when we apply this approach to specific important social issues.

Some of what is relevant here has already been considered. It was argued in Chapter 4 that religious intolerance and persecution reflect an absence of empathic concern for fellow citizens (or fellow inhabitants of a given country), and I was already willing at that point to say that this shows religious intolerance and persecution to be unjust. But the present chapter's explicit treatment of the conditions of social justice makes it clearer, I think, why a claim of injustice can be said to follow from facts about the motivational bases of intolerance and persecution, as we historically and presently know them.

We have also seen, however, that not every interference with civil liberties or freedoms need be considered unjust. As I argued in Chapter 5, a refusal to allow certain kinds of hate speech may not proceed from, or reflect, a lack of empathic concern for fellow citizens, and so our empathy-based criterion of justice will tell us that such a refusal, such an interference with liberty, needn't be unjust (or violate anyone's rights). On the other hand, and as we also recognized earlier, patriarchal social attitudes can embody a lack of empathic concern and respect for the aspirations of girls and women (for example, to become doctors), and we can say that all laws, customs, and institutions that reflect such attitudes are as unjust as the attitudes themselves (and the situation in which they flourish).

Similarly, women who work outside the home have typically ended up doing more total work than their husbands, and this too can be considered a form of injustice (or unfairness). For if women have to do an inordinate amount of the work that needs doing in their families, that fact reflects social expectations or attitudes that embody a failure of empathy and concern for women's needs and aspirations: for example, the widespread view that women have to take primary responsibility for childrearing and housekeeping *whatever their role outside the home may be*. It may be convenient for men to go along with such attitudes because it gives them more free (leisure) time than they might otherwise enjoy, but a willingness on the part of husbands to overburden their wives in this way constitutes great selfishness toward those they are supposed to love and, commensurately, a great *lack* of empathic consideration for – or fairness toward – their wives. So the view of justice that we have derived here from the ethics of empathic caring *condemns* any situation in which full-time working wives do a great majority of the work of caring within families – rather than encouraging or colluding in the oppression or injustices that women have traditionally suffered or presently have to endure.[5]

The case just mentioned illustrates the way in which public attitudes can have unjust repercussions in the private or family sphere (though the causal influence needn't run just one way). But in fact a comprehensive ethics of empathic caring needn't put much (or any?) moral weight on the whole distinction between the personal/private and the political/public. Both realms are to be judged in terms of empathic care, and there is no reason, for example, why the unfair or unjust distribution of work within families shouldn't be a subject for political consideration and amelioration: perhaps legislatures need to pass laws mandating compensation, by their husbands or partners, for women who do a disproportionate amount of housework or caring for children. But this is to raise issues of distributive justice.

2. Distributive Justice

A society is just to the degree or extent that its laws, institutions, practices, attitudes, and customs are just, and we have offered a specific criterion for when laws, etc. are just in terms of ideals of empathic caring that apply at the level of social groups. We have been applying that criterion here – I hope successfully – to a large number of issues, but I think that it works well for *all* questions of social justice. The most important issue of justice that we haven't yet considered relates to poverty and equality. Our theory needs to be able to say something plausible about the justice or injustice of serious inequalities of wealth, and this is precisely what I propose to do here. However, it may help in doing this if we first say something briefly about the distribution not of wealth, but of political power.

In some societies a ruling elite denies most people a political voice, a vote, and we consider this a paradigm of injustice.[6] But the injustice can be unpacked in care-ethical terms, because the refusal to grant basic political privileges or rights always – I really think always – expresses and reflects a rather greedy and selfish desire, on the part of the elite, to retain their hegemony of power, privilege, and (typically, though not always) wealth. This constitutes far less empathic concern for (the welfare of) one's compatriots than would be reflected in a fully developed capacity for empathy with others, and so our approach will deem such a situation (politically) unjust.

Now similar criticism can be made of a meritocratic society in which there is no (guaranteed) safety net for the handicapped, the poor, or the unemployed. Even if such a society allows everyone to vote, a power elite may successfully oppose all proposals to provide economic help for the handicapped, etc., and it is plausible to suppose, once again, that such opposition reflects or exhibits a selfishness and greed on the part of the elite that is incompatible with a level of empathic concern for the worst-off members of society that seems well within our human capacities. To be sure, meritocracies have their ideologies, as do monarchies that deny the people all political power: one can refuse people help in the name of what one calls libertarian ideals, as one can preserve exclusive political power by referring to the divine right of kings. And if this sounds more than slightly Marxian, that is not, I think, a reason to run away from what I am saying here. Marx may have been wrong about many, many things, but what he said about our tendencies to rationalize self-interest or sheer selfishness in the name of ideology rings true to many of us who take a strictly democratic approach to the political realm. And it may ring especially true to feminists (and women) who have, for example, seen scripture cited for the purpose of justifying patriarchal attitudes and institutions. So I think we need not hesitate to draw the conclusion that a refusal to pass laws instituting a social safety net counts, for reasons having to do with empathy or its absence, as an economic form of injustice.

But of course it is possible to hold that injustice(s) of an economic kind can exist even when a social safety net is in place, and I would like now to spend some time considering that possibility. A safety net is compatible with enormous differences of wealth and with a considerable amount of poverty, and an ethics of empathic care that turns its attention to issues of (distributive) justice may well want to suggest that justice requires *more* than a safety net, that it requires that the rich and those with high incomes be taxed *more steeply* than those at the lower end of the economic scale. Considerations of marginal utility offer us, in fact, a very good moral reason for preferring and instituting the kind of progressive taxation on the rich and those with high incomes that makes for greater economic equality within society as a whole.

Given decreasing marginal utility, when we tax a rich person's money, we typically do less harm than when we tax a poor person's money. But, even more importantly, when we tax rich or high-income individuals for the benefit of those who are poorer, the latter tend to gain a great deal more than the former lose. This fact gives us some empathic grounds to favor redistributive progressive taxation, and I believe the justice of progressive tax legislation and the injustice of not instituting such taxation can both be accounted for in care-ethical terms. But we need to be careful here. When we tax rich or high-income individuals (or anyone else), we either take money they already have, or actively prevent them from receiving certain moneys, but what we said in

Chapter 3 entails that we are empathically more sensitive to causing harm (or something bad) than to merely allowing harm (or something bad) to happen. We shy or flinch from maiming or harming a person, even if that is the only way we can bring about a greater amount of good for people, and if the acts of a just government express empathic concern for the governed, doesn't that mean a government should hesitate to cause harm or make things worse for people than they otherwise would be? Isn't this, in turn, some sort of reason for governments not to tax the rich for the benefit of the poor? (I take it that it *isn't* a reason for governments to avoid taxation altogether.)

In the empathic care-ethical terms discussed in Chapter 3, it is indeed such a reason, but that doesn't mean the reason can't be overridden. After all, most deontologists think it can be permissible to harm or even kill someone if the benefits of doing so are great enough, and the benefits of progressive taxation clearly are great. Because of diminishing marginal utility, the harm redistributive progressive taxation does to the rich is enormously outweighed by the good it does for those who are poor or not well off, and I think empathic concern for fellow citizens would not in fact make legislators 'flinch' from instituting various forms of progressive taxation. Quite the contrary. And so our theory can regard such taxation as just, and even as required by justice.[7]

However, nothing we have said indicates that justice requires, or even allows, the progressive tax rate to be as steep as possible, so that society comes progressively closer (excuse the pun!) to complete socio-economic equality. The highest or steepest rates of taxation and any general insistence on equality, or near-equality, of wealth or income might very well deprive people of incentives to work hard, and quite possibly would make society as a whole lose greatly in economic terms. The latter fact is (also) one to which empathic caring is or would be sensitive, so our account of justice needn't insist on the highest rates of progressive taxation, and would instead claim that the issue of how steep progressive taxation should be has to depend on empirical considerations.[8] But there is a further, very interesting complication that also needs to be mentioned at this point.

Utilitarians often make use of considerations of marginal utility to argue for progressive taxation, but in addition they hold that the rate of taxation shouldn't be so steep as to diminish overall economic output (or overall social utility). However, the utilitarian also holds that justice requires the passing of laws that do a great deal (only) for those who are already well off, when the only alternative is legislation that would do somewhat less good for those who are poorly, or less well, off, and this will seem morally unacceptable to most of us. Rawls's difference principle (in A *Theory of Justice*) is intended precisely to avoid what utilitarianism is counterintuitively committed to here[9], but I want to argue that the ethics of care can also handle this issue more intuitively than utilitarianism does. This requires a bit of explanation.

Imagine a young person, z, who lives in such conditions of poverty and deprivation that he is always painfully hungry, though he is not, in fact, in danger of actual starvation or serious malnutrition. An older person, x, comes along and, seeing z's situation and having greater resources of her own, arranges for z to have enough food now and in the future so that he will never again feel such painful hunger. At some later time, another person, y, comes along and discovers that z is actually very bright and talented. Y arranges for z's admission to a fine college and pays both for the college and for z's subsequent attendance at law or dental school. The rest of the story can, I believe, be told in such a way that we could reasonably conclude that y had actually helped z *even more* – had done him *even more* good overall – than x had.

This case involves, of course, two agents successively helping a single person. But, given what we have just said about it, we can consider next a situation in which one agent has to decide which of two possible recipients of his aid to help. Either u can help relieve v of perpetual feelings of hunger (what x did for z), or u can make it possible for another person, w (who is not feeling hunger), to attend college and dental or law school and have the opportunities that all this will predictably bring as a result (what y did for z).

I think most of us, if put in u's position, would be inclined (other things being equal) to help a person in v's situation rather than help someone in w's; and the reason has to do with empathy. We tend to feel more empathy and empathic concern for someone whose situation or condition is a bad one than for someone whose situation or condition is merely not wonderful, and this difference can mean that we prefer to help the former even if we are in a position to do somewhat more good for the latter.[10] Our ethics of empathic care entails, then, that we should take both marginal utility and (what we can very, very roughly call) absolute positionality into account in determining what is moral or just; and since legislators (and framers of constitutions) whose empathy is fully developed will have greater empathy and a special/greater concern for those in their society whose position is bad or terrible (or will be, if nothing is done to help them), our theory of justice mandates a much higher degree of economic equality than utilitarianism provides for.

Put another way, our view requires legislation and institutions that don't reflect a lack of compassion, for compassion is clearly sensitive to what I am calling absolute badness (for individuals).[11] (How hungry one feels and other aspects of what is bad for people may depend partly on the comparisons one makes with how others are doing, but I think the reader can understand, nonetheless, what I mean by talking of absolute badness here.) We feel more empathy for, and have more tendency to act on behalf of, those who are in bad shape or circumstances, and the term 'compassion' takes in that aspect of empathy – we wouldn't call someone compassionate if they wanted to do somewhat more good for those in acceptable circumstances rather than some-what less good for those in horrible circumstances.[12]

However, compassion also includes an empathic tendency to respond more to those in immediate danger or misery – where both perceptual and temporal immediacy are meant. I mentioned earlier, for example, that the person (like

Fried; see Chapter 2) who preferred to install safety devices rather than help contemporaneously trapped miners would show himself to be less than fully compassionate. I am now saying that, in addition to being responsive to temporal and also perceptual immediacy, the compassionate person has to be responsive to the sheer badness of someone's situation. But all these are factors we are empathically sensitive to, so we can conclude that compassion marks out a particular subset of the factors that empathy is responsive to.[13] We can thus say that a kind of social compassion, or at least laws and institutions that don't manifest a lack of compassion, are a necessary condition of social justice according to an ethics of care.[14]

Now we have been concentrating for some time on the motives of legislators and others toward those who live in their own country. But many will hold that a just society, with just laws and institutions, will not be indifferent or hostile to the interests of people in other countries, and that certainly seems to be correct. However, a theory of justice that stresses empathy should have no problem in addressing these issues. Just as morally decent individuals develop an empathic concern for people (who they don't personally know) living outside their own country, fully developed empathy on the part of legislators will take in the wellbeing of people in other countries. Such legislators will presumably be less concerned with citizens of other countries than with citizens of their own – the ethics of empathic care is not impartial like utilitarianism – but the legislation they approve (for example, the level of humanitarian foreign aid they support) should at least reflect a substantial amount of concern for the welfare of people in other countries (and for the welfare of the countries themselves considered in aggregate terms); and the theory I have offered can explain why, on grounds of justice, this ought to be so.[15]

There are other political/legal issues that an ethics of care will want to address: most notably questions of criminal and tort justice that we really haven't dealt with here.

But I think it would be better if I took up these issues elsewhere and at a later date, and in any event what we have been saying in this chapter should give a pretty good idea of how care ethics would approach such further questions. The ethics of care clearly doesn't have to confine its attention to personal morality and relationships: it can speak of social (including legal and economic or distributive) justice in its own terms and what it has to say will seem plausible, if the care-ethical approach to personal or individual morality is seen as plausible. If anything, the account of the justice of institutions and laws sketched here should make the ethics of individual caring seem *more* plausible by showing that its basic approach needn't be confined to individual matters, but can be extended to cover large-scale moral issues as well.

However, there is an important aspect of the ethics of care that we still haven't said much about. The ethics of care is a form of sentimentalism and is clearly not a form of rationalism – that much I indicated earlier in the book. But I haven't yet considered the specific question whether an ethics of care can, or should, say that it is rational to act morally. I would like to take up that question, and then consider the more general issue of what it means to act or behave rationally, in Chapter 7.

Notes

1 In Chapter 5, it was argued that morally acceptable action may also require an agent to be unwilling to impose things on another person when there is no chance that the other person ever will, or would, accept their having done so. But this condition isn't relevant to the present discussion, and I shall simplify matters by not mentioning it in what follows.

2 What I am saying about particular laws also applies, *mutatis mutandis*, to the framing and ratification of a constitution. Note, too, that the motives and beliefs that keep a law in existence may also be relevant to its moral assessment. But I shall leave this complication to one side.

3 I assume that we can assess group motives (to a large extent) on the basis of the motives of the individuals in the group, but there will certainly be cases – e.g. where a group is closely divided in its motives and attitudes – where group attribution is a delicate, or sometimes even a vague, matter. In such instances, according to what I have been saying, it is difficult to assess a law morally, but given care ethics, individual acts whose motivation is ambivalent or murky can also be difficult to evaluate. Since all theories allow for hard cases, this doesn't seem to be a particular problem for a care theory of justice. (I am indebted here to Scott Gelfand.)

4 In *Morals from Motives* (Michael Slote, *Morals from Motives*, New York: Oxford University Press, 2003) I assumed that national legislation should express equal concern for all citizens, but it is difficult to make sense of this in terms of empathy. However, even if national legislators are more concerned with their own constituents (and especially their own families and themselves), they may be motivated by substantial concern for the good of their country, and in that case the laws they pass will be just in care-ethical terms.

5 Recently available evidence shows that this problem may have existed more in the past than it does today, at least in the USA. S. Bianchi, J. Robinson, and M. Milkie (*Changing Rhythms of American Family Life*, New York: Russell Sage Foundation, 2006) report that, although wives still do twice as much childcare and housework as their husbands, the amount of childcare and housework done by fathers has increased sharply since 1965, and the total hours of work done by mothers and fathers are now roughly equal.

6 This is less clear in primitive societies and tribes where those who don't rule never think to ask for a role in ruling.

7 Does this mean that, where there are no governmental provisions for redistribution and there are enormous disparities in wealth or income, it can be all right and even good for private individuals to redistribute wealth forcibly by stealing from the rich in order to give to the poor, or even in order to alleviate or mitigate their own miserable circumstances? My answer is a tentative, hesitant 'yes', that it can be morally all right. But if enough people take matters into their own hands, that can threaten the stability of society, and although threats to the stability of certain societies can be a good thing (as in the case of justified revolutions), a group that threatens social stability can have a lot to answer for. There is no reason, however, why this cannot be unpacked in empathic care-ethical terms.

8 One relevant consideration is how much alienation or solidarity is felt within a given society. Where there is solidarity and/or mutual empathic caring among citi-

zens, hard work may be compatible with mandated economic equality. But this is a complex issue (cf. G. A. Cohen, 'Incentives, Inequality, and Community', reprinted in S. Darwall, ed., *Equal Freedom*, Ann Arbor, MI: University of Michigan Press, 1995, pp. 331–97).

9 John Rawls, A *Theory of Justice*, Cambridge, MA: Harvard University Press, 1971.

10 The idea that one should help those badly off, rather than do (somewhat) more good for those not badly off, can be found e.g. in Harry Frankfurt, *The Importance of What We Care About*, Cambridge: Cambridge University Press, 1988, Ch. 11; Joseph Raz, *The Morality of Freedom*, Oxford: Oxford University Press, 1986, Ch. 9; Derek Parfit's Lindley Lecture 'Equality or Priority', Lawrence, KS: University Press of Kansas, 1991; Roger Crisp, 'Equality, Priority, and Compassion', *Ethics* 113, 2003, pp.745–63. Only Crisp stresses empathy as a basis for this moral preference, and these authors disagree among themselves in various ways about whether one should favor worse-off people who are not badly off in absolute terms, and about other issues relevant to the value of equality. I don't take sides here on these further issues, because I think the relevant deliverances of both empathy and of morality itself are somewhat unclear. This is an important topic, however, for further investigation and elaboration. But let me just add that Rawls's difference principle (A *Theory of Justice*, *ibid.*) clearly doesn't focus on absolute badness, but rather on relative position with respect to primary goods. It would be interesting to consider how the view offered here differs from Rawls's in regard to particular social situations, but again I think this should be left to another occasion.

Finally, I would like to make use of what we have been saying to respond to an interesting criticism of my views about deontology that can be found in Michael Brady's 'Some Worries about Normative and Metaethical Sentimentalism', *Metaphilosophy* 34, 2003, pp. 148f. I argued in Chapter 3 that the fact that empathy reacts to causal immediacy helps to justify our belief that it is worse to kill than to let die. But Brady notes that we are also in a more causally immediate relation to benefits we cause rather than merely allow, and he asks how I can avoid the conclusion that we may permissibly kill (or cause grievous harm) if that is the only way we can cause greater benefits to others. However, given our greater empathic sensitivity to what is absolutely bad for individuals, it should be clear why we would prefer not to kill or cause *grievous* harm for the sake of conferring greater benefits on those who are not, and are not in danger of being, badly off. Moreover, we will be reluctant to kill one person even to save a couple of worthwhile lives because, once again, the death one would bring about is an absolutely bad thing for a given individual, whereas when one preserves a life, what one brings about is at best 'merely' good. (I am indebted here to Scott Gelfand.) Note, however, that if the ill imposed isn't absolutely bad or dire, common-sense deontology is more willing to allow a trade-off for greater positive benefits: one can permissibly deprive someone of property in order to save a life or a limb, and progressive taxation is also defensible in this light.

11 Crisp ('Equality, Priority, and Compassion', *op. cit.*) makes the same point.

12 Incidentally, questions about *how many* people are going to be affected can complicate the moral issues we are dealing with here, so I ask the reader to assume, for simplicity's sake, that the same number of people are affected whichever choice one makes in the cases I am discussing.

13 For reasons I don't fully understand, a preference for a greater number of strangers over a lesser number of family members or friends yields the accusation that one lacks true love or true family feeling, or a true sense/feeling of friendship, but doesn't evoke the criticism that one is lacking in compassion. Similarly, someone (who is merely) not sensitive to the difference between doing and allowing doesn't get accused of lacking compassion.

14 On the moral and political importance of compassion, see Martha Nussbaum, 'Compassion: The Basic Social Emotion' in Ellen Frankel Paul, Fred Miller Jr, and Jeffrey Paul, eds, *The Communitarian Challenge to Liberalism*, Cambridge: Cambridge University Press, 1996, pp. 27–58. On the role of empathy in understanding political and legal issues, see Jane Mansbridge, 'Feminism and Democratic Community' in John Chapman and Ian Shapiro, eds, *Democratic Community: Nomos* XXXV, New York: New York University Press, 1993, pp. 347–61; Diana Meyers, 'Social Exclusion, Moral Reflection, and Rights', *Law and Philosophy* 12, 1993, pp. 125f.; and Martha Nussbaum, *Poetic Justice*, Boston, MA: Beacon Press, 1995, pp. 79–121.

15 Given what was said in Chapter 4, *respect* for the citizens or inhabitants of other countries doesn't require as much empathy as does respect for fellow citizens or compatriots.

7

CARING AND RATIONALITY

Advocates of care ethics such as Nel Noddings see caring as grounded in feeling. They look to Hume as a forerunner of their approach, and it is natural to regard them/us as moral sentimentalists.[1] But the original sentimentalists, unlike most Kantians and liberals, thought that their view left morality, moral behavior, unjustified in rational terms. Both Hutcheson and Hume hold that it is not irrational, not against reason, to do immoral things, and they also hold, more generally, that there is no such thing as practical rationality. Even given its roots in and affinity for sentimentalism, does or should a care ethicist accept either or both of these further assumptions? (I say 'further' because to claim that moral actions depend on feeling, and that moral judgments are justified by reference to facts about feeling, is not quite yet to have committed oneself to the strong views that Hume and Hutcheson hold about rationality.)

In what follows, I want to argue that an ethics of empathic caring has no reason to try to avoid Hume and Hutcheson's assumption that immorality needn't be (considered) irrational. That assumption, or conclusion, is not as dangerous or implausible as many ethical rationalists have believed, and I want to explain why I think this. On the other hand, I do think we have reason to resist the extreme sentimentalist claim that there is no such thing as practical – as opposed to theoretical – rationality; and I want, later in this chapter, to sketch a positive account of practical rationality that sits well with our caring approach to morality. Finally, I shall want to say something here about the place of reason or rationality within care ethics as a whole, and about how the care-ethical ideal of fostering caring relationships fits in with what has, or will have, been said earlier in this chapter.

1. Is Morality Necessarily Rational?

I see the claim that acting morally is rational(ly required) as different from the claim that there are reasons for being moral. It is possible to construe the latter as saying that certain judgments or beliefs about what it is right or obligatory for one to do can be supported by good reasons – by considerations that justify the judgments or beliefs about rightness or obligation; and this seems, from the standpoint of care ethics, to be a fairly unobjectionable thing to say. But even if we can justify moral claims, it doesn't follow that it would be irrational for us not to follow the dictates of morality. From the fact, assuming it is one, that it is wrong to torture people, we can't immediately conclude that it would be or is irrational for us to do so. In that case, the question whether morality is rational (is rationally required of us) is still up in the air, and from the standpoint of our care ethics, that means we have not yet been given any reason to think that someone who acts in a way that expresses or reflects a lack of empathic concern for others is acting irrationally. The question, then, is whether a care ethicist can or should accept such a conclusion.[2]

Now most rationalists clearly won't accept the conclusion, but since the present approach takes issue with rationalism at many points, that is no reason in itself why *we* should hesitate to accept it.[3] We have to consider whether there is any argument for thinking of morality as a rational requirement that doesn't presuppose some form of ethical rationalism (but that might then be used to *support* rationalism). Here is one such argument that emerges from Bishop Butler's discussion of conscience.[4]

Butler claims that conscience *presents itself* as rationally authoritative over us, and if he is right about the phenomenology here, then there certainly seems to be some reason to think that it is irrational to go against the dictates of conscience – presumably, and other things being equal, there is always some reason to think that things are as they appear to be. In that case, if we assume that conscience doesn't err in what it tells us are our obligations, we are rationally required to act morally, and care ethics – given its emphasis on how things feel – will be hard pressed not to agree.

But *does* conscience, the judgment of conscience, really have or convey the appearance of rational authority that Butler thinks it does? When a person is influenced or goaded by conscience to do something, does this come in the form of a warning telling one that it would be irrational not to do the thing? When someone is bothered by her conscience for not having done something, is the voice of her conscience like someone telling her that she has been irrational? *Pace* Butler, I think all these questions have to be answered in the negative. Conscience tends to induce anxiety, fear, guilt, and self-loathing;[5] but the idea of rationality or irrationality doesn't seem to be included in its intentionality. (In a recent discussion of Butler's views on conscience and its rational authority, Stephen Darwall also expresses doubts about whether conscience actually presents itself to us as rationally authoritative.)[6]

So Butler doesn't give us any good reason for thinking that morality is rationally required of us, and at this point I would like to offer an argument for the opposite conclusion. The argument isn't based on phenomenology, but rather on what seem to be intuitively plausible (or commonsensical) assumptions about what morality involves. I believe there is at least some intuitive reason to think we are *not* rationally required to be moral, and I also think what has been and can be said on behalf of a caring approach to morality serves to reinforce this initial intuition. Let me explain.

Normally, it is considered irrational for people not to care about their own welfare. But we don't think it irrational not to care about the welfare of others. Thus the statement 'it is irrational/foolish of you not to care what happens to him, because you know perfectly well that you need his help' makes immediate intuitive sense; but a statement like 'it is irrational/foolish of you not to care what happens to him, though nothing that happens to him can have any good or bad effect on you' would normally leave the hearer baffled or awaiting some further explanation. And that is because there is a more immediate or intuitive tie between rationality and self-interest than between rationality and the interests of others. But, of course, our concern for the interests, the welfare, of others is a central part of almost any morality: there are many occasions when it is morally obligatory to help others, and on many other occasions it is at least morally praiseworthy for one to do so. So, at least intuitively, it doesn't seem implausible to deny the irrationality of acting immorally or being immoral, but it does seem implausible to deny the irrationality of acting against self-interest or of lacking concern for one's own wellbeing. (Actually, we intuitively regard it as irrational not to be concerned with one's own *long-term* self-interest, wellbeing, or happiness, but I shall frequently drop this qualifier or specification in what follows.)

What has just been said doesn't in and of itself *prove* that morality isn't a requirement of rationality and/or that self-interested prudence is, but it does show that such views have a *prima facie* plausibility and deserve serious consideration. Later on, I want to defend further the idea that concern for one's own (long-term) wellbeing or happiness is a condition of being (a) rational (person). But at this point I think it is important to consider how the intuitive, commonsensical notion that it is not irrational (in itself) to act immorally or be immoral sits with our ethics of empathic care.

We have already said that care ethics counts as a form of sentimentalism because of the crucial and basic role it gives to feeling. Now presumably care ethics recommends caring and thinks it is wrong not to act in a caring way (I am speaking roughly here); but if care ethics doesn't say that uncaring motivation and actions are irrational, *does it then have enough to say against (what it takes to be) immorality?* Well, in addition to accusations of uncaringness, the care ethicist can also criticize (actions that display) certain sorts of indifference and hostility to others as *heartless*, and that is a very strong thing to be able to say.[7] In fact, in many ways it feels a lot stronger than the accusation of irrationality, though it is perhaps no stronger than impugning someone's rationality on a given occasion by saying they have done something *stupid*. But the point is that we are now assuming that the care ethicist is tempted to say that (accepted, true) moral claims aren't rationally binding, that all or the most we can say against someone who is immoral or acts immorally is that they are heartless. This may indeed be a strong claim but, given the philosophical issues that surround morality, is it *enough*?

Moral philosophers often speak of the *normativity* of moral judgments, and there is fairly widespread agreement among philosophers that moral claims or judgments *are* normative. But normativity is sometimes conceived as rational force or authority, and I have already denied, or at least doubted, that morality is normative in that sense.[8] So is there any other plausible understanding of normativity that would allow care ethics to subscribe to the fairly compelling and (in the field of philosophy) widespread idea that moral judgment is (in some important sense) normative? One could try saying that the normativity of morality simply resides in the fact that moral claims are genuinely evaluative claims and make practically relevant *recommendations*. But I don't think this is really quite enough. What we need to be able to say is that moral claims are *categorical*, are categorical imperatives in Kant's sense; and if care ethicists can say such a thing, I think they will have subscribed to an appropriate level or sense of normativity. But can they?

What might persuade one that they can't is the thought that Hume and the other eighteenth-century sentimentalists lacked Kant's distinction between hypothetical and categorical imperatives. And, indeed, Hume doesn't draw that distinction – as far as I know, Kant was the first philosopher to do so explicitly. But it doesn't follow that the distinction wasn't implicit in what Hume said about morality, any more than the fact that ordinary people haven't explicitly made the distinction means that it isn't implicit in *their* moral thought and practice. After all, in making the distinction between categorical and hypothetical imperatives, Kant appealed to our ordinary, everyday understanding of (the great force of) morality; his distinction merely brings out what is implicit in that understanding and in our practice. And there is similar reason to think that Hume does or can regard moral claims or utterances as categorical imperatives in the Kantian sense. This point has been made very eloquently with respect to Hume by David Wiggins, so I don't want to pursue here the particular question whether Hume's moral views are consistent with allowing moral utterances to have a categorical character.[9] What I do want to say, though, is that there is no reason why a care ethicist should deny or want to deny that the moral judgments s/he subscribes to are categorical in Kant's sense.

According to Kant, someone to whom a hypothetical imperative is addressed can plausibly beg off by arguing that she lacks the relevant desires or motives. But, on the Kantian view, the absence of desires, motives, or intentions relevant to the fulfillment of a categorical moral imperative doesn't leave the person to whom it is addressed outside the scope of that imperative – doesn't make the imperative inapplicable to that person in the way that can be true for hypothetical imperatives. Now according to care ethics, it is or can be wrong for me not to help, say, my daughter, even if I have no desire to help her. But if the relevant moral judgment of obligation applies to me and makes me liable to moral criticism even if I lack the relevant desire, then that judgment is functioning as a categorical imperative within care ethics.[10] So sentimentalism, and care ethics in particular, can treat morality as genuinely normative, even while denying that moral judgments are either based in reason or rationally binding.

But if we can't give a rational justification for being moral, as the care ethicist seems to hold, isn't that fact a regrettable one? Wouldn't it be better, wouldn't we prefer it, if we could somehow show that someone who acts immorally is irrational to do so? Well, in one sense, perhaps, it would be better if we could show this. For then we might just be able to persuade immoralists to mend their ways and to act in a morally better fashion than many of them do. And arguably most of us have a stake in, have something to gain from, such people's moral improvement. For similar reasons, it might also be preferable if we could show that morality is in the self-interest of the morally decent individual, and such a conclusion, if it could be made persuasive, might be even better for getting immoralists to change their ways than merely convincing them that immorality is irrational.

But from the standpoint of someone who care ethics regards as a morally good or decent individual, these things, these conclusions, may not be at all relevant or important. Prichard famously argued that the attempt to justify morality by reference to self-interest takes us beyond, and in some sense runs counter to, ordinary moral thinking (and acting).[11] Someone who thinks he morally ought to do something doesn't typically worry or wonder about whether doing that thing would be to his advantage or in his own self-interest, and I would expand or extend Prichard's point by adding that such a person also typically doesn't wonder whether it would be irrational of him to act immorally. The attitude of someone who sees something as his clear duty or obligation treats such rational or self-interested considerations as extraneous and, by-and-large, irrelevant.

Moreover, and once again expanding Prichard's point so that it now takes in the morally unselfconscious attitudes and motives that care ethics prizes, we can say that someone who is motivated by love or friendship or other caring motives to do something for someone is also going to treat the above rational and self-interested considerations as extraneous and irrelevant. In fact, if she does see them as relevant, if she worries or wonders seriously whether what she is doing for another person is in her self-interest or for some other reason rationally required of her, the assumption that she loves or deeply cares about the other person will be criterially undercut to a certain extent. She will count as loving or caring to a lesser degree than if such considerations or questions about rationality and self-interest didn't (tend to) concern or worry her. (This is really just a continuation or expansion of points made earlier in Chapter 5.) So I conclude that, although it might be nice to be able to persuade immoralists that it is in their self-interest or that it would be rational for them to mend their ways, the idea that morality is in our self-interest or is rationally incumbent on us plays no essential role in the moral life of moral individuals. And neither, furthermore, does it have to play a role in moral education, since the process of induction described by Hoffman doesn't require a parent to bring in issues of practical rationality or self-interest, and can rely mainly on the child developing concepts and empathy. But we now have to consider whether care ethics can or should have anything positive or constructive to say about practical rationality *outside the sphere of morality*.

2. Views of Practical Rationality

Historically, moral sentimentalism has been skeptical or nihilistic about (what rationalists have taken to be) the role of practical reason or rationality. As I already mentioned, Hume and Hutcheson don't think morality can be grounded in, or shown to be a requirement of, practical reason, but both also doubt whether there is *any such thing* as practical rationality: they doubt its existence even *outside* the sphere of morality. Hume seems to be the more consistent, and the more skeptical or iconoclastic, of the two, because while both agreed that reason is exclusively theoretical (concerned with determining truth and falsehood), Hutcheson also claims that it is *reasonable* to try to obtain as much as we can of what our instincts direct us toward, and *unreasonable* not to.[12] In contrast, Hume thinks there is nothing contrary to reason in preferring the lesser of personal goods, and holds that it is never motives or actions that are unreasonable, only *judgments*.[13] Even with respect to instrumental rationality, Hume seems to be committed to thinking that willing or intending an end without choosing or intending an appropriate means can, at most, involve some sort of intellectual error.

So it is probably a mistake to think of Hume (the way so many have) as espousing an *instrumental conception of practical reason*, and this might well give pause to a contemporary sentimentalist like the care ethicist. The irrationality of (roughly) willing an end without willing the means is not usually regarded as just being a matter of irrational *judgment*, and I think it would do irreparable damage to the present-day case for sentimentalism, and for care ethics, if such views had to be combined with a Humean denial of the possibility of practical reason/rationality. However, we wouldn't face this problem, or be in such hot water, if it could be shown that the practical irrationality of willing the end without willing the means is reducible to (or can be eliminated in favor of) a certain sort of inconsistency of judgment, and R. Jay Wallace has recently defended such a view.[14] So let us see if Wallace's argument can persuade us that Humean views of practical rationality are less unpromising than one might have initially thought.

According to Wallace, instrumental rationality just consists in having consistent beliefs. If you intend to do X, believe doing Y to be a necessary means to doing X, but fail to intend to do Y, then your irrationality consists in the fact that you hold the following inconsistent set of beliefs:

(1) It is possible that I do X.
(2) It is possible that I do X only if I also intend to do Y.
(3) I do not intend to do Y.

But is the instrumentally irrational person really committed to all these beliefs, and are they (the beliefs s/he is committed to) really inconsistent? Let us look first at belief (2). (2) contains an ambiguity in the scope of the modal operator that has to be clarified before we can tell whether the instrumentally irrational person is committed to a real inconsistency of beliefs. Given wide scope of the operator, (2) means that it is not possible that I do X without also intending to do Y. And if the circumstances are 'normal' ones in which one cannot do X accidentally or by mistake, then under this wide-scope interpretation, (2) is true and presumably believed by the irrational agent. However, there is another interpretation of (2) under which the modal operator has narrow scope and (2) means something like: If I never intend to do Y, then doing X is not (is never) a possibility for me. But on this reading, (2) is seemingly false and there is no reason to think that the instrumentally irrational person has to believe it. In normal circumstances, something can be a possibility for me, can be within my powers, even if I never intend to do it or to pursue the sole means of doing it: as long as I can or could intend these things. For example, I have never intended to buy wind chimes, but it has long been possible or in my power to do so.

Now if we interpret (2) with narrow scope, then as I just said, the instrumentally irrational person isn't committed to believing (2). But if we interpret (2) as having a modal operator with wide scope, then even though the irrational person will be committed to believing (2), *there is no inconsistency among (1), (2), and (3)*. All three will in fact be *true*. I don't intend to take the means to buying wind chimes, it is not possible that I buy them but never intend to take any means to buying them (like going to a relevant store); but it is possible that I buy wind chimes (this is something within my power). Wallace fails to see the scope ambiguity in (2), but once one does, it should be clear that the instrumentally irrational person isn't committed to an inconsistent set of beliefs. Wallace's neo-Humean approach doesn't seem to work, and if we find an outright denial (*à la* Hume) of the possibility of practical rationality to be implausible, the care ethicist and the sentimentalist more generally are left with an interesting choice.[15]

It might be possible for the (care-ethical) sentimentalist to argue, for example, that morality cannot be understood in rationalistic terms, but that there is something properly called practical reason that exists (somewhat) independently of morality and that can in fact best be accounted for in terms familiar to rationalism. This would put rationalism, so to speak, in its place, but it would give it more of a place than Hume allowed it. Care-ethical moral sentimentalism would then be *just* that: a view that excluded any rational basis for morality, but that in no way excluded the possibility of understanding practical rationality in some other sphere or spheres (for example, with respect to the agent's own good) in rationalistic terms.

In that case, ethics as a whole would have to include a sentimentalist care-ethical view of morality supplemented by a rationalistic account of non-moral practical rationality. But now the reader may be wondering why the practical rationality that exists outside or independently of morality couldn't instead *be understood in sentimental terms*. Morality and rationality may be different and independent of one another, but that doesn't in itself entail that rationality can't be understood sentimentally; the most it could mean would be that practical rationality has to be understood in *different* sentimental terms from those that help us understand the nature of morality. If morality can be understood in terms of empathic concern or caring, why couldn't practical rationality rest on different, for example self-interested, sentiments?

Perhaps, in fact, it could, but the issue is somewhat complicated. If there is to be such a thing as practical rationality, then it has to set standards or requirements that the rational or human agent may either meet or fail to meet. So an account of practical rationality in terms of sentiments other than caring, empathy, love, and the like cannot simply say that being rational is a matter of doing what we want or desire the most. If reason is, in this sense, so thoroughly a slave of everyone's actual passions, then reason doesn't set a standard that passion/desire, and action based in such, can meet or *fail to meet*. And in that case there is no such thing as practical rationality. Practical rationality as such must embody a standard in the light of which the actual can be criticized, rather than giving *carte blanche* to whatever people want. So a conception of practical rationality tied to actual sentiments in a thoroughgoing way cannot give us a sentimentalist account of practical rationality capable of supplementing what care ethics says about the sphere of the moral.

The point can be illustrated specifically in regard to instrumental rationality. Someone may (let us assume) 'will' a single solitary end without willing/intending the necessary means to that end, and Kant famously considers this to be irrational. But if actual desire is the criterion of practical rationality (so that reason is the slave of the passions), then it wouldn't be possible to criticize such a combination of sentiments and/or their absence as irrational. Since we presumably do want to criticize such a combination of desires/attitudes, we have to get beyond the (Humean-like) criterion of actual desire(s), and it is difficult to see how any *sentimentalist* criterion of practical rationality could actually allow us to criticize means/end irrationality.[16]

We can say, if we want, that there is some kind of *conflict* between a desire for the end and the absence of any desire for the means, but such conflict isn't in fact reducible to any kind of sentiment. For the conflict we are talking about doesn't amount to any kind of feeling pulled in two directions, as happens when we speak of psychological conflict, and in fact the person who wills the end without willing the means may not feel any psychological conflict. We may indeed want to criticize him for that, to be sure, but the criticism isn't based on the idea that someone who wills the end and doesn't will the means should feel conflict about it; on the contrary, such a feeling wouldn't (much) undercut the irrationality involved in such cases, because what we find irrational in cases of instrumental irrationality is chiefly the fact that the person wills the end and doesn't will the means. What we most object to is not the absence of a conflictual sentimental reaction to that fact, but the fact itself.

We are inclined to say, for example, that anyone who wills an end without willing the means is (in some sense) practically inconsistent. But such claims express a rationalist view of instrumental rationality, rather than accommodating or helping sentimentalism in this area. The accusation of practical inconsistency is a mainstay of Kantian moral argument, and we can see the tendency toward rationalism that is built into such ideas if we remember that inconsistency isn't a sentiment that one can either exemplify or fail to exemplify. Intending or desiring something may be, in some sense, a sentiment, but to say there is an inconsistency between desiring/willing/intending one thing and not desiring/willing/intending another, is not to speak of some further sentiment. Rather it is to criticize a certain combination of sentiments in what clearly seem to be rationalist terms. Inconsistency is, first and foremost (or most familiarly), a cognitive or theoretical vice, something to be avoided in the area of belief (formation); so if we are committed to criticizing someone's willing an end without willing the means, and think that what is wrong here can be insightfully characterized as some form of inconsistency, then we arguably have a rationalist view of what is involved in instrumental rationality, not a sentimentalist one.

Perhaps we should be content with that. Perhaps sentimentalism understood as care ethics can best account for the moral, but *rationalism* offers us the best way to understand practical *rationality* (understood as operating independently of the moral realm). That would be an interesting and far from disheartening conclusion for the present book to reach, and I mention it, in part, because it represents something we might want or need to fall back on, if the sentimentalist approach to practical rationality I am now going to propose ultimately fails.[17] But at this point, I would like to propose a sentimentalist account of practical rationality that anchors it in a certain kind of sentiment that is different from those crucial to morality, and that doesn't take the rationalist route of treating consistency/inconsistency as a major element in understanding practical reason.

3. Rational Self-Concern and Instrumental Rationality

If morality revolves around the sentiment/motive of empathic concern for others, then perhaps practical rationality derives from the sentiment/motive of *self*-concern. The latter is not, presumably, centered or based in any kind of empathy (although it seems possible to feel empathy, for example, for one's much younger self); but the kind of cognitive development necessary to the

development of full empathy with others has its parallel in the growth of pru-
dential thinking. And certain levels or degrees of self-concern, of concern for
one's own (long-term) welfare, represent a *standard* of practical rationality
because not everyone is self-concerned in those ways, and people thus lacking
in self-concern can then be *criticized*. If we can work out an acceptable account
of practical rationality in relation to the motive of self-concern, then we really
will have a sentimentalist account of practical rationality. But this is by no
means an easy thing to do, because doing so requires us, among other things, to
show how means/end rationality can be subsumed under the rationality of self-
concern; and *that* is not easy. Or at least it is not obvious. But let us begin by
saying more about the rationality of concern for one's own wellbeing.

Morality requires us (roughly) to act in ways that don't exhibit a lack of the
sentiment/motive of empathic concern for (the welfare of) others; but for reasons that I stated earlier, and that are intuitive enough in themselves, being
practically rational requires us to act in ways that don't show us to be (totally)
lacking in concern for ourselves, for our own welfare. For just as someone who
lacks concern for others is morally criticizable, someone who lacks (an appropriate degree of) concern for himself can be criticized as being (an) irrational
(person). I shall say more about what is appropriate here later in this chapter,
but the point that needs to be stressed now is that, if we can subsume all other
issues or aspects of practical rationality under the rational imperative of long-
term self-concern (or long-term self-interest conceived as a motive, not a
desired result), then we really will be able to offer a sentimentalist theory of
practical rationality.

To that end, I am going to argue now that instrumental rationality can be
understood as an aspect of (rational) concern for one's own wellbeing or happiness in contexts where the wellbeing or happiness of others is not a salient
issue. Rather than claim, rationalistically, that someone (in such a context)
who wills or seeks his own happiness, but doesn't take the necessary means to
it, is inconsistent, I want to say instead that such a person simply doesn't value
his own happiness enough. In other words, the motive of self-concern is less
strong or fully developed than practical rationality requires if, in contexts
where other people's happiness isn't a major issue, one doesn't will the necessary means to one's own happiness. But this claim remains entirely within the
terms available to sentimentalism, since it argues or assumes that instrumental
irrationality is irrational because it demonstrates a lack or a lesser degree of a
certain sentiment.[18] Just as someone who says they are concerned with another
person, but who doesn't make any effort to find out what the person needs (or
who is slapdash and careless in trying to promote that person's welfare) shows
herself to that extent to have less deep or full concern regarding that other
person, so too does someone who intends his own happiness as an end, but is
unwilling to pursue (or is slapdash about) the necessary means to that happiness show himself to have (rationally) deficient concern for his own happiness.
If instrumental rationality can be understood along these lines, then perhaps

we can be sentimentalists about practical reason generally, but there may be a problem here.

After all, not all putative instances of instrumental rationality or irrationality occur in the context of the rational pursuit of self-interest, and it is important for any sentimentalist account to be able to handle the full range of cases involving the taking or not taking of means to ends. The rationalist considers the failure to take necessary means to ends to be irrationally inconsistent, and such inconsistency exists irrespective of the particular ends a given agent has. Thus although, for Kant, it is a mark of irrationality to will/intend gratuitous harm to someone, a person who fails to take the necessary means to the harm he intends is *doubly* irrational. But the sentimentalist can't say that all failures to take means to ends are irrational, and can say this only about cases where such failure indicates a lack of rational self-concern. The requirement that one take means to ends is thus, for the sentimentalist view of rationality we are exploring, a merely *conditional* requirement, one that operates only in the context of the pursuit of self-interest, and is this consequence really acceptable? Well, let's examine it in a specific instance.

Imagine someone whose end is the good of another person, but who, because she is deflected from that end by strong self-interested desires, doesn't take a necessary means to the original end. Because we naturally tend to think of self-concern as a rational motive and tend not to regard helping others as rationally incumbent on us, it is not so clear what we should say about this case. Certainly, the person who is deflected shows herself to be less morally good, less devoted, than we might have hoped. But is it so clear that what she ends up doing is *irrational*, rather than simply criticizable in moral terms?

Let's consider another example, one not involving any morally desirable ends. Imagine someone who has a dominant but arguably irrational goal in his life and who sometimes doesn't take the necessary means to furthering that goal. It could be someone, for instance, who wishes to spend all his time counting blades of grass in 'geometrically shaped areas such as park squares and well trimmed lawns', but who on certain occasions unaccountably fails to count the blades of grass in such areas.[19] Is this irrational, or, more precisely, does the failure to count on a particular occasion, given the general life goal and the absence of other ends, represent *an additional failure of practical rationality beyond that involved in having the general goal in the first place?*

The answer is not obvious, and that is because in isolation from rational goals or ends, the rational significance of taking or not taking necessary means is much less clear-cut or obvious. This suggests that (the force of) instrumental rationality may not be independent of the particular goals an agent is pursuing, but, rather, is subsumable under the rational imperative to seek one's own good, or welfare, or happiness, as our sentimentalist approach says. Where a goal or end is irrational, the failure to take means to it is not a further irrationality, I suggest, but is either neutral from a rational perspective or perhaps even rationally commendable or positive, because it shows one to be less committed to the irrational goal than one might have been. Thus if I am bent on buying myself cigarettes, but unaccountably (at the last minute or persistently) fail to take the means to doing so, then I may in fact count as *less* irrational than if I do take that means,[20] and in any event the irrationality of wanting and intending to get cigarettes in the first place arguably isn't *compounded* by the failure to take a necessary means to that irrational end.

If we take this line, then perhaps instrumental or means–end rationality can be understood in sentimentalist terms. We will no longer say that all failures to take the necessary means to one's ends (in the absence of other reasons, etc.) are irrational because they involve a certain inconsistency between elements within one's own psychology. Cases like those of the grass-counter and of the person who wants cigarettes seem to most of us to be less-than-clear examples of instrumental (or twofold) irrationality, and the sentimentalist wants to say that that fact is due to the irrationality of the basic goals of the agents described in those examples. If that explanation is granted, then not all failures to pursue means to ends are irrational, and such irrationality, whenever it *does* occur, will be attributable to the insufficient strength of a certain, rationally required sentiment, namely self-concern. But consider, then, finally, what this means about the sort of case described earlier, where someone has the goal of helping another person but for self-interested reasons fails to take the means to that goal. If what I have been suggesting is correct, then such a person also isn't acting irrationally, and any tendency we have to insist that they are derives mainly from the rationalist/Kantian assumption that helping others is a requirement of practical reason, an assumption the sentimentalist presumably doesn't share.

Now everything the sentimentalist can say about means/end rationality they can also say, *mutatis mutandis*, about weakness of will, or akrasia. (For reasons we needn't go into, not all cases of weak will involve a failure to take a means to an end.) In other words, I think the sentimentalist can make a case for holding that weakness of will, in the sense of not doing what one thinks best to do and/or what one has set oneself to do, is only conditionally irrational and, in particular, is irrational only when it demonstrates a deficiency of rational motivation, of self-concern. This goes against received or traditional ideas about weak will,[21] but what I have said in favor of a sentimentalist view of means/end rationality (as conditional) also favors a sentimentalist view of weakness of will (one could use variants on many of the examples I used above to make the case). What I want to say, then, is that if – *if* – one has good reason to accept a sentimentalist care-ethical account of (individual and political) morality, there is reason to accept a sentimentalist view of practical rationality as well. Its implications for particular cases are not implausible, and it is good, on theoretical grounds, to pursue sentimentalism consistently across different areas of ethics.

4. Caring versus Self-Concern

In the previous section, I suggested that individuals are practically rational (in sentimentalist terms) only if they are motivated to pursue their own long-term happiness in contexts where the good of others is not a major issue.[22] But this doesn't tell us how much or how strongly one is rationally required to pursue happiness in such contexts, and, perhaps more importantly, it also doesn't tell us what it is rational to do in situations where one has to *choose between* helping oneself and helping others. We need to consider both these questions.

According to the care ethics developed here, an acceptably or decently caring individual has fully developed empathic concern for others, so if someone cares only about her own wellbeing or happiness, then she is clearly not a morally decent person, even if she counts as perfectly rational. However, even if care ethics tells us that it is bad or unvirtuous to be totally selfish or indifferent to others, it *doesn't* tell us that we have to be selfless, that is, totally unconcerned with our own wellbeing.[23] The (or a) full development of the human capacity for empathy and empathic concern for others doesn't extirpate self-concern, but rather occurs against a background of natural and persisting concern for one's own welfare. Increasing empathy may limit or attenuate that self-interested motivation, but on the other hand such motivation is a natural (or inevitable or normal) element in human beings that can set limits to *how much* we can feel empathy and be concerned with others.[24] So morality conceived in the present care-ethical terms doesn't require a total absence of self-concern, but this still leaves open the all-important question whether the full development of empathic concern for others requires us to be *less concerned with our own welfare or happiness than rationality requires*. In other words, is morality (being a moral person) compatible with rationality (with being a practically rational person)?

Given what has been said so far, it is not obvious that it is, and also not obvious that it isn't. I said earlier that a moral, caring person isn't totally selfish, in the sense of caring only about his own welfare, of being indifferent to the welfare of others. But it is possible not to be selfish in this sense while never being willing to sacrifice one's own welfare to that of others, and I think caring requires in fact a willingness to make some such sacrifices. A person who is fully empathic with and concerned about others will sometimes give up something that she wants in order to help another person gain something good. Such a person may give up a pleasant night at a concert in order to care for a sick friend, for example, and in such a case, at least for ordinary ways of thinking, one sacrifices one's own good for that of another. But does this entail that one is being irrational? It all depends on *how much* concern for one's own good or happiness is required for someone to count as practically rational.

Let's be commonsensical about this issue. We don't, in fact, necessarily think of someone who makes sacrifices for others as irrational. In particular, we tend not to think of this as irrational if the person *also* seeks his own happiness to a substantial extent. So selfishness and an unwillingness to sacrifice for others don't seem to be necessary to being practically rational, but an absence of selflessness does, and no intuitive incompatibility between morality and practical rationality has yet appeared. On the other hand, certain other sacrifices, however praiseworthy in moral terms, do seem rationally suspect. The soldier who throws himself on a hand grenade rather than, like his fellow soldiers, diving for cover is and should be morally praised. But his mother, while being proud of what he has done, might also think it was foolish or irrational for him to have thrown his life away (even for such a noble cause). But since throwing yourself on a hand grenade is a plausible example of going beyond the call of duty, we still don't have a case where being moral and being rational turn out to be in conflict. (It wouldn't have been immoral for the soldier to have dived for cover like everyone else.)[25]

However, we also have to consider how strongly self-concern operates in purely self-regarding contexts in an individual who is rational. If only one's own long-term welfare or happiness is at stake, can it be rational, for example, to pursue it less than maximally? In previous work I have argued that it indeed can be, that someone who seeks good things needn't seek to have as much of them as possible.[26] To count as practically rational, I think one need only have a moderately strong concern for one's own long-term happiness, a concern that doesn't require one always to maximize one's good or wellbeing in self-regarding contexts. And if such moderate self-concern is all that is required for rationality in self-regarding contexts, that makes it easier to understand how practical rationality can allow one to sacrifice one's (greatest) good in other-regarding contexts.

As for the rational requirements to be instrumentally rational and non-akratic, these occur, as I said earlier, in relation to the rational imperative(s) of self-concern. So what I am saying now is that particular instances of akrasia, or a failure to take the necessary means to an end, are irrational only if they display or evince an overall lack of the moderate self-concern that I am claiming is (all that is) required for practical rationality in an individual. Just as a person shows herself to lack fully developed empathic concern for others if she fails on a given occasion to respond to a child drowning right in front of her, so too can a person show a lack of personal rationality if, say, he on a given occasion doesn't bother to take medicine that he thinks may be (a) necessary (means) to his survival or continuing good health. Such a person shows a lack of the kind or degree of concern for his own long-term happiness or wellbeing that seems intuitively to be necessary to being practically rational. And, of course, the very fact of the intuition shows that a sentimentalist account of practical rationality conceived in terms of the sentiment, or motive, of self-interest or self-concern has a great deal going for it.

The picture we end up with, then, is of the practically rational individual as someone who has and shows substantial concern for her own happiness in contexts not involving others, and whose self-concern isn't entirely washed away in contexts where the welfare of others is at stake. Such a person won't be selfless, but they may be willing to make sacrifices for others (even perhaps when what they sacrifice of their own welfare is greater than what they obtain for or give to others). Morality may not be required by rationality, but it seems perfectly consistent with the substantial but far from all-encompassing self-concern that practical rationality, conceived in intuitive sentimental terms, seems to require. And if we can account for rationality and its relation to morality in sentimentalist terms, that further supports the care-ethical conception of morality defended in the earlier chapters of this book.

Now most care ethicists focus not only on what is good for individuals or groups of individuals, but also on (the partially overlapping issue of) what makes for good relationships. The caring individual is supposed to be concerned with the welfare of other people, but also (and overlappingly) with the building and maintenance of good caring relationships; and, as I indicated earlier, many or most care ethicists think that the goodness of caring relationships constitutes a more basic ideal than caring as an attitude, virtue, or motive. However, I have already said that I don't think we need to decide this latter issue in the present context. What we do need to understand better is how the ideal of caring relationships fits, or fails to fit, with what we have previously been saying, in terms of the notion of empathic caring, about our moral obligations and (more implicitly) about moral virtue.

The first thing to notice, in this connection, is that those who are engaged (together) in building or maintaining a caring relationship are typically motivated by a mixture or combination of egoistic (self-concerned) and altruistic (caring) motives. Given, therefore, what has been said up to now in the present book, and especially in this chapter, we can say that caring relationships are motivated by both rational and moral considerations, and this means, I think, that caring as a relational ideal is not *exclusively* a moral ideal. I am inclined to hold, in other words (and we have been implicitly assuming something like this all along here), that morality – both in the form of moral virtue and in the form of moral obligation or duty – centers around the empathically caring concern to promote the welfare of other individuals or groups of individuals. To the extent, therefore, that the goal of (co-)building certain relationships involves a desire to promote *one's own* wellbeing and/or non-welfare-related, perfectionist motivations, it is not a specifically moral goal, even if it is directed toward something that we can (in the broader sense of the term 'ethical' that most of us are familiar with) call ethically ideal, or at least good.[27]

The criterion offered earlier in terms of empathic caring was a moral criterion, a criterion of moral permissibility, and when I spoke of supererogation, I was again speaking in specifically moral terms. In that sense, too, the empathically caring individual can be characterized as possessing (a) moral virtue, and I think it is fair to say that the present book has been primarily interested in the moral aspects of the ethics of care. I am not sure that all or most care ethicists would be comfortable with my way of singling out the moral side or dimension of care ethics, or with the more general distinction I am relying on between the moral and the ethical. But, allowing myself that distinction, I want to say that the care-ethical recommendation that we build and sustain caring relationships (a recommendation that one finds in work by Noddings, Held and others, and that I don't want to dissent from) is not specifically a moral one. What *is*, I think, specifically moral is the empathic concern or effort to make other people (or animals) better off,[28] and to the extent that such a desire is involved in the building and sustaining of relationships, the latter task, or joy, involves moral elements or aspects. But I believe these can be accounted for in the same empathic-caring terms that our book has empha-sized. Similarly, when relationships are bad or far from ideal, that can be because (as I described in Chapters 4–6) they exemplify a lack, or distortions, of empathic caring (or worse) and are thus criticizable in specifically moral terms, for example as unjust or unfair. But (possibly at the same time) the badness can also be due to non-moral problems, failures or inadequacies: a relationship in which people aren't able to enjoy themselves or to work very efficiently together can be bad or less than ideal – but not necessarily because of moral considerations.

However, a further point needs to be made. Where love exists between two individuals, it may be difficult to draw a sharp distinction between their inter-ests, between what promotes the welfare of the one and what promotes the welfare of the other. This needn't make us claim that there is no distinction between the two individuals or that one is literally part of the other. (The fact that this kind of thinking is often associated with substitute success syndrome should certainly give us pause.) But where or if interests blur in this way, cer-tain potential conflicts or tensions between rational and moral concerns may be softened or undercut. If I work evenings to make enough money to send my child to medical school, I may be *ipso facto* promoting my own long-term hap-piness, not just my child's. In that case, a moderately strong concern for one's own good may (sometimes) involve or allow for more concern for others than would perhaps be rational, if promoting the good of another person could never constitute a way of promoting one's own good.[29] But, either way, it is a certain level of self-concern that is essential to individual practical rationality, so the considerations just mentioned do nothing to call our sentimentalist account of practical rationality into question.

At this point, finally, I would also like to speak a little more generally than I have previously about the place of reason in care ethics, and the first, possibly the most important thing, to say is that reason *has* a significant and substantial place within the ethics of care. Care ethics may reject moral rationalism and hold that morality isn't based on reason; it may reject the traditional ethics of justice in favor of its own self-standing view of morality; but this is not at all tantamount to a rejection of reason, rationality or, for that matter, thinking. Sentimentalism and rationalism about morality are, after all, contrary views, contrary theses about the basis of morality. And traditional justice ethics turns out, as we have seen, to have implications that contradict what a developed ethics of care wants to say. But (the importance of) reason/rationality/thinking and (the importance of) emotion/feeling are not contrary or contradictory in this way. It is often said – usually by men – that women are (more) emotional and men (more) rational, but even this (vague) claim, if true, wouldn't entail that women don't (think or feel that they) need reason, rationality and thinking itself; and in any event ethicists of care typically regard reason, thought and rationality as useful and important to human life and to morality.[30]

Thus, even if morality isn't based on reason, there is no reason to suppose that moral individuals, as conceived by care ethics, have no need for their rational, or reasoning, powers. A mother who cares about her child wants to know how to do what is good for her child, and this involves knowing and initially learning all sorts of nutritional and medical facts, just for starters. One learns and retains such facts better if one is rational, reasonable, about gathering and weighing evidence, but notice that this kind of reason/rationality is not specifically practical (though it serves practical purposes). The mother's rational weighing of evidence is of a piece with – or at least connected to – what natural and social scientists do, and so I am saying that theoretical and epistemic (as opposed to practical) rationality is and has to be very much involved in the life of the caring individual. In deciding what to do, say, for a child, a parent needs a substantial degree of epistemic rationality, and the ethics of care can and should insist on this point. Moreover, to the extent that a parent is careless or slapdash about finding out what his or her child needs, their love or caring is substantially impugned or undercut, and so various attitudes and desires *vis-à-vis* the (learning of) facts can be criticized in care-ethical moral terms.

Now Kant and many Kantians tend to assume that (the agent's) emotions aren't relevant to moral decision-making, but the fact that care ethicists disagree with this doesn't mean they reject all uses of reason and rationality in determining what should be done in a given situation, or in general.[31] They do, however, see abstract or universal rules or principles as less morally useful or usable than Kantian rationalists do, so the kind of reason(ing) and thought they think is relevant to morality is, to some extent, different from what Kantians or others have traditionally assumed.[32] On the other hand, consider how cognition is relevant to empathy. As I pointed out in Chapter 1, the fullest sort of empathy with other individuals requires an ability to see them as individuals, which children have to acquire. The use of language and the development of certain concepts are relevant to our capacity for empathy, so an ethics of care that emphasizes empathy has every reason to insist on the importance of cognitive development and, therefore, on the role of (non-practical) reason or thinking within the moral life.

But not just there. Anyone who thinks and makes claims about the ethics of care has to place a value on theoretical reason and reasoning, even if, as I mentioned in Chapter 1, they don't want to claim that moral, caring individuals need to pay attention to care ethics as a theory or account of morality. It would be self-thwarting indeed if care ethicists sought to articulate a (partial or systematic) ethics of care, but denigrated the rational or reasoning capacities that are (I think clearly) required for the doing of philosophy and social science.

In the end, therefore, the contrast that an ethics of care draws between reason or thinking and emotion needn't be exclusive or exclusionary in the way that the contrast between sentimentalism and rationalism, which are mutually contradictory views, has to be seen. Care-ethical sentimentalism may not think that practical reason grounds morality, but it has, or can have, its own distinctive conception of practical reason, and it allows great scope and use for other kinds of reason and reasoning within morality, and in human life generally.[33]

Notes

1 Nel Noddings, *Caring: A Feminine Approach to Ethics and Moral Education*, Berkeley, CA: University of California Press, 1984, esp. p. 79.

2 Nel Noddings (*Caring, op. cit.*, pp. 25, 61f.) clearly doesn't regard caring as any sort of rational requirement.

3 Almost everyone will grant that it is, at least occasionally, irrational to do what is immoral – sometimes acting morally is the only prudent thing for someone to do. Also, it is frequently argued on empirical grounds that it is always in our interest to be moral and act morally, but the question before us is whether there is something in itself or inherently irrational about acting immorally, and empirical issues are not directly relevant to *this* question. In other words, we are asking whether there is something in itself or inherently irrational about acting uncaringly or being uncaring, and we don't yet have any sort of answer to this question. Of course, there is also the issue whether immorality or uncaring behavior necessarily goes against *self-interest*, but the typical modern rationalist holds that we are rationally required to be moral independently of whether immorality usually or necessarily goes against self-interest, and that is the view that I believe care ethics can and should call into question.

4 Bishop Butler discusses conscience both in his *Fifteen Sermons* and in *The Analogy of Religion*. See J. H. Bernard, ed., *The Works of Joseph Butler*, London: Macmillan, 1900.

5 To the extent that conscience induces fear and anxiety, it has a phenomenology similar to what *de facto* authorities often induce or create in us, but it is a long stretch from there to the conclusion that what is operating in either case is the embodiment of a certain kind of rationality.

6 Stephen Darwall, *The British Moralists and the Internal 'Ought': 1640–1740*, Cambridge: Cambridge University Press, 1995, p. 283.

7 'Cold' might be a good term for the care ethicist to use to characterize the attitudes and actions of someone who is indifferent to other people, but the term doesn't seem apt for malice and misanthropy and acts that display those motives/attitudes.

8 Stephen Darwall (*The British Moralists and the Internal 'Ought', op. cit.*, pp. 247–72) is one among many who understand normativity in this way.

9 David Wiggins, 'Categorical Requirements: Kant and Hume on the Idea of Duty', *Monist* 74, 1991, pp. 83–106, esp. pp. 91f. Wiggins offers an interesting account of why critics may have thought that Hume and the other sentimentalists were incapable of allowing for categorical imperatives.

10 My usage of 'categorical imperative' is pretty close to what Kant says about the notion when he introduces it in the *Groundwork*. But Kant also believes that only moral 'oughts' are categorical, and that such 'oughts' constitute rational requirements, and I am not making either of those assumptions. Philippa Foot ('Morality as a System of Hypothetical Imperatives', reprinted in S. Darwall, A. Gibbard, and P. Railton, eds, *Moral Discourse and Practice*, New York: Oxford University Press, 1997, pp. 313–22) argues that Kant needs or wants a stronger sense of 'categorical imperative', one that entails reason-giving force. But she allows that imperatives are normative when they are categorical in the sense I have been using, and that assumption is precisely what I need for the argument given in the text.

11 H. A. Prichard, 'Does Moral Philosophy Rest on a Mistake?' in his *Moral Obligation*, Oxford: Clarendon Press, 1949.

12 See Hutcheson's *Illustrations of the Moral Sense*, section I, and for further discussion of both Hutcheson's and Hume's views in this area see Stephen Darwall, *The British Moralists and the Internal 'Ought'*, op. cit., esp. pp. 319ff.

13 See Hume's *Treatise* (L. A. Selby-Bigge, ed., *A Treatise of Human Nature*, Oxford: Clarendon Press, 1958, esp. pp. 416, 458). For a somewhat different take on Hume, see Peter Railton, 'Humean Theory of Practical Rationality' in D. Copp, ed., *The Oxford Handbook of Ethical Theory*, New York: Oxford University Press, 2006, pp. 265–81.

14 R. Jay Wallace, 'Normativity, Commitment and Instrumental Reason', *Philosopher's Imprint* 1, 2001: www.philosophersimprint.org/001003

15 Sigrun Svavarsdottir is working on a neo-Humean approach to practical reason that avoids the above criticisms of Wallace's view and that (unlike Hume) makes room for a genuine notion of practical rationality. When her paper 'The Virtue of Practical Reason' is completed, it will be interesting to see whether it can accommodate, or be accommodated to, a sentimentalist ethics of caring.

16 Bernard Williams, 'Internal and External Reasons' (in his *Moral Luck*, Cambridge: Cambridge University Press, 1981 and elsewhere) has defended what he calls an internalist conception of practical reasons, arguing, among other things, that what we have reason to do is relative to our actual motivational set, and that moral obligations that are external to an agent's motivational set in the way that rationalist/Kantian moral theories require are philosophically problematic. But Williams allows one to have reason to do something, even if one doesn't want to do it, as long as there is a 'sound deliberative route' from the set of one's actual motivations to the act in question. What he has in mind here is that someone who wills an end without willing the necessary means has, but doesn't take, a sound deliberative route to willing that means, and can be criticized on that basis. But this is, in some sense, externalist, because it imposes a standard of criticism on what someone may actually desire, and doesn't treat reason as the slave of our actual set of passions. In that case, it is not clear why morality too shouldn't be able to impose external(ist) demands allowing us to criticize what the agent desires or chooses.

17 The agent-based account of practical rationality I previously developed (Michael Slote, *Morals from Motives*, New York: Oxford University Press, 2003, Ch. 7) focused to some extent on inconsistency and was to that extent rationalistic – even though I was offering a sentimentalist virtue theory of morality and also treated the sentimentally understandable motive of concern for one's own welfare as part of what is required for someone to count as rational. Clearly, it is possible to be a sentimentalist about morality and a rationalist about practical reason – this would be a new and distinctive kind of ethical dualism; but the present book presses the general case for sentimentalism further or harder than I did in the earlier work.

18 In the *Groundwork of the Metaphysics of Morals*, Kant assumes that one *can* will an end without willing the means, and that if one does so, one is being irrational. But one might question whether it really *is* possible to will an end without at all willing or being concerned to bring about the necessary means. For example, Christine Korsgaard ('Skepticism about Practical Reason', *Journal of Philosophy* 83, 1986, pp. 5–25) points out that failure to take available means to stated ends can make it somewhat doubtful whether those really are a given person's ends. However, she goes on to suggest that whether one takes means to ends one really has may (simply) depend on how practically rational one is, and similarly, in an essay commenting in part on Korsgaard's views, Stephen Darwall says that there is no (factual, as opposed to rational) guarantee that someone desiring some goal will have motivation for an acknowledged means to it. What I am saying in the text above, however, is that even if one doesn't make the strong claim that someone who doesn't will the means doesn't really have or will the end, one can still (and contrary to what Korsgaard and Darwall imply) make the plausible weaker claim that if someone intends or wills an end but not the means, that entails that the person either doesn't intend the end at all, or intends it *less intensely or less fully* (other things being equal) than someone who intends or wills both an end and the necessary means. (For Darwall's view, see his 'Reasons, Motives, and the Demands of Morality: An Introduction' in S. Darwall, A. Gibbard and P. Railton, eds, *Moral Discourse and Practice*, New York: Oxford University Press, 1997, p. 309. For claims somewhat similar to those I am making here, see Thomas Hurka, *Virtue, Vice, and Value*, New York: Oxford University Press, 2001, p. 107; R. Jay Wallace, 'Normativity, Commitment and Instrumental Reason', *op. cit.*, p. 26; Nomy Arpaly, *Unprincipled Virtue: An Inquiry into Moral Agency*, New York: Oxford University Press, 2001, Chs 2 and 3, esp. p. 100.)

19 The example is borrowed from John Rawls, *A Theory of Justice*, Cambridge, MA: Harvard University Press, 1971, pp. 432f. However, Rawls is less willing to call such a basic life goal irrational than most of us, I think, would be.

20 I have recently learned that Nomy Arpaly makes something like this claim in her *Unprincipled Virtue*, *op. cit.* However, for defense of the more traditional view that those who fail to take means to ends they consider bad are additionally irrational, see R. Jay Wallace, 'Normativity, Commitment and Instrumental Reason', *op. cit.*

21 Both Donald Davidson ('How Is Weakness of the Will Possible?' in Joel Feinberg, ed., *Moral Concepts*, Oxford: Oxford University Press, 1969, pp. 93–113) and David Pears (*Motivated Irrationality*, Oxford: Clarendon Press, 1984) seem to hold that weakness of will or akrasia is always irrational. But I don't believe either counts as an ethical rationalist overall.

22 One issue I won't discuss in any detail is how *self-consciously* or *explicitly* a rational person pursues his or her own happiness. It seems possible that someone should pursue happiness without *thinking specifically about happiness*, and while simply seeking good things (for herself) that she would acknowledge as (potential) elements in her happiness *if* she were asked about this. The same point also applies to altruistic examples such as concern for the welfare of one's children.

23 Starting in Chapter 4, we saw that care ethics can be very critical of situations, attitudes, and actions that lead people to become selfless or self-abnegating. But it is perhaps worth making the further point that someone who has been made selfless may actually (unconsciously) resent or be angry about what has happened to them, even if they say they place a great value on (their) selflessness. This may tend to show that they are in fact *less* selfless than they or others say or think they are, that their self-interested motivation has been distorted, thwarted, and suppressed, rather than extirpated or rationally/morally argued out of existence. What I am saying will, I hope, strike a familiar and resonant chord with readers, and if it does, that shows

how much more suspicious we are of selflessness than the Victorians were. We think that a person who says he wants only to serve others may be simply fooling himself and may actually resent (some of) the others. Or we suspect that such a person serves other people out of irrational or inordinate guilt feelings, amounting perhaps to a form of masochism. To that extent, we are inclined to rule out (actual, genuine) selflessness as a possible human development, holding, rather, that some degree of self-concern may be inevitable even in human beings (like certain Victorians and Buddhists) who have strived or claim to be selfless, or who say they see selflessness in certain other people.

24 Martin Hoffman (*Empathy and Moral Development: Implications for Caring and Justice*, Cambridge: Cambridge University Press, 2000) describes a number of different ways in which 'normal' self-interest or self-concern sets limits on how much empathy for others we can develop or display.

25 Perhaps we have such a case if we imagine someone who has to choose between saving her own life and saving thousands of other people. But even here, one can wonder if the sacrifice is actually morally required; and it is also possible to question whether sacrificing one's own life for the sake of thousands shows an irrational lack of (normal) self-concern. For highly relevant discussion of such issues, see Derek Parfit's forthcoming *Climbing the Mountain*.

26 Michael Slote, *Beyond Optimizing: A Study of Rational Choice*, Cambridge, MA: Harvard University Press, 1989.

27 I also want to leave open the possibility that self-regarding (rational) considerations and other-regarding (moral) ones may, in some cases, be so entangled or inter-penetrating that we cannot specify them separately. This may happen when people share goals, activities, or interests (a point I get from Nancy Sherman); but, as we are about to see in the main text, it can or might also happen when one person is especially devoted to, or concerned about the welfare of, another person. I don't think any of this is threatening to what I have been saying here.

28 Remember that our ethics of empathic caring sees (even) deontology as an aspect or modality of the concern for human welfare.

29 For helpful relevant discussion, see Grace Clement, *Care, Autonomy, and Justice*, Boulder, CO: Westview Press, 1996, Ch. 2.

30 Thus Carol Gilligan ('Moral Orientation and Moral Development' in E. Kittay and D. Meyers, eds, *Women and Moral Theory*, Totowa, NJ: Rowman & Littlefield, 1987, p. 20) says that the distinction between the justice perspective and the care perspective cuts across the distinction between thinking and feeling.

31 Care ethicists are typically open to the idea that emotion and reason can affect or permeate one another, but I don't think this is the place to investigate the meaning, implications, or validity of this suggestion. More generally, feminist epistemology is highly relevant to the issues I am touching on and summarizing here, but again this doesn't seem the right place for a discussion of feminist epistemology.

32 On this last point, see Virginia Held, *The Ethics of Care: Personal, Political, and Global*, New York: Oxford University Press, 2006, p. 11.

33 Martha Nussbaum (*Sex and Social Justice*, New York: Oxford University Press, 1999, pp. 74ff.) says that care ethics exalts emotion over reason, and thereby denies women the critical apparatus to call into question and change invidious social attitudes and institutions. Her primary target is Nel Noddings's book *Caring* (*op. cit.*); but whatever may be the validity of what she says about Noddings, her criticism doesn't apply to an empathy-based care ethics. Such an ethics may not base morality in reason, but it allows reason a very substantial role in moral life and thought; as we have amply seen, such an ethics itself formulates criteria of respect, justice, and morally acceptable behavior that allow women, or anyone, to criticize patriarchy.

CONCLUSION

This book has attempted to show that distinctions of empathy broadly mark or correspond to plausible moral distinctions, and I have also been saying that empathy is crucial to moral motivation. It doesn't seem as if these facts can be accidental, and that is a reason for regarding facts about empathy or, better, empathic caring as justifying various (particular) moral claims. But even if we have reason to treat empathic caring as criterial for individual and political morality, we may still want to know *why* empathy is relevant to right and wrong, justice and injustice, and in this conclusion I would like to say something about this issue. To get us started, let me just briefly discuss some reasons that have been given for thinking empathy *can't* be basic or central to morality.

In 'Empathy and Animal Ethics', for example, Richard Holton and Rae Langton mention the possibility that we might have difficulty empathizing with the pain of extraterrestrials, if the pain they felt was very different from anything experienced by us and/or was signaled by external behaviors very different from the signs of pain among animals here on Earth.[1] According to them, that would make no difference to our obligations to relieve (what we knew to be) their pain(s), and they cite this as a reason for denying empathy a major role in grounding moral thought and action. I wonder, however, whether they would be so sure of this if they considered the moral difference empathy seems to make to our actions regarding pain in other instances. Perhaps, on something like utilitarian grounds, they would deny that it is all right to be more concerned with pain one perceives than with pain one merely knows about. Perhaps they would deny the moral relevance of immediacy altogether, and would reject the considerations of shared lives and natural empathic responsiveness that seem, intuitively, to be so relevant to our greater obligations toward intimates and toward those whose suffering or danger is contemporaneous with our moral decision-making (remember the miners example). But someone who *doesn't* reject such considerations, and who accepts what we said here in earlier chapters, might well then question Holton and Langton's treatment of extraterrestrial examples.

For such a person, it wouldn't be morally repugnant and unacceptable – or very surprising – if we were more concerned about pain that we could 'read off' from, or see in, someone's behavior than about pain, even in an extraterrestrial being right before our eyes, that we knew to exist only on the basis of indirect evidence and arguments. Even if reading off and seeing involve some sort of (unconscious) inferences based on evidence and argument, there is a phenomenological distinction here, and our earlier chapters, especially Chapters 1 and 2, in effect offer a defense of such phenomenology as relevant to empathic responsiveness and, therefore, as a basis for moral distinction-making. (I know no less well that there are children I can save from pain by giving money to Oxfam than that I can alleviate the pain of a child I see suffering right before my eyes. The difference is in how that knowledge presents itself to me.) So assuming that the extraterrestrials really are in *pain*, I am claiming that the indirectness of our knowledge of such pain would arguably make some difference to its empathic immediacy for us and to our obligations in regard to it. In the light of our whole argument here, it doesn't seem implausible to say such things, and so I don't think Holton and Langton's example of extraterrestrial pain has any tendency to undercut the idea that morality is based in or centered around empathy. But let me now mention one other objection to this idea that has recently surfaced.

Contemporary ethical rationalists like Thomas Nagel and John McDowell have argued that moral action doesn't have to be motivated by feeling(s) or desire(s), but can be explained as resulting from the perception or understanding of certain relevant facts. But I don't believe such rationalists ever claim that morally good action can occur *in the absence of* empathy, even if their approaches don't treat empathy as a central or basic factor in morality.[2] Now the present book hasn't directly engaged the arguments that have been offered in favor of ethical rationalism, and I don't propose to start doing that at this late point. But I think we might do well to consider the seemingly rationalist position Jeanette Kennett takes specifically about the relevance of empathy to moral judgment and action.

In 'Autism, Empathy, and Moral Agency,' Kennett argues that autistic people (especially those with the 'high-end' form of autism known as Asperger's syndrome) may be capable of moral judgment and action, despite their inability to empathize with other people and their consequent inability to respond to many morally significant social cues.[3] But we need to look into this issue very carefully. Some autistic people may, for example, be capable of empathy even if they lack the ability to respond to certain social cues: the empathy that responds to certain kinds of immediacy may require such an ability, but an empathic concern for whole groups of people may possibly not. Also, many autistic people demonstrate a remarkable affinity for and emotional connection with animals, and that, too, may make one question whether they really are totally incapable of empathy. Finally, the examples Kennett uses to illustrate the moral capacities of people with Asperger's syndrome make the responses of such people seem (to me) based more on the desire to fit in with or please those around them, than on what most of us think of as genuinely moral motivation. In any event, we need to look into autism and Asperger's more deeply, and these phenomena may represent good test cases for the issue between rationalism and care-ethical sentimentalism. But without further evidence and argument, I don't think autism and Asperger's syndrome yet constitute a major argument against forms of ethics that are centered around empathy.

However, even if, on the basis of all that has been said, we have strong reason to suppose that empathy is deeply involved in or relevant to morality, we still don't have any explanation of *why* this should be so. If we had a plausible definition of 'morally good' or 'morally right', that might help us to such an explanation, and perhaps the easiest way to imagine such an explanation working would be to imagine the term 'empathy' or one of its cognates actually occurring in the definition of these terms. Now, as I mentioned earlier, the word 'empathy' wasn't even invented until the twentieth century, but I don't think that means the notion of empathy can't have played a role in our thinking before that time, or that it couldn't have been involved in the concept of moral rightness or goodness that existed before the twentieth century (I am speaking loosely, but I hope understandably). Even if we didn't have a name for it before the twentieth century, empathy was a known phenomenon earlier on, and Hume, Adam Smith, and other eighteenth-century figures make reference to and seem to understand the phenomenon of empathy, even if they didn't have that particular term for it.

It is plausible to suppose, in addition, that educated, sensitive readers understood what Hume and Smith were talking about when they described what we now call empathy, so the concept of empathy may not have been foreign to our thinking before the twentieth century. In that case, the concept of empathy might have been involved in the concept of rightness or goodness even when we didn't have a word for it, and there is all the more reason, then, to conjecture that it may play a role in the concept of rightness we work with at present, given that we have a term for it now, and are now always talking about people being or not being empathic/empathetic. I am not saying that terms like 'right' have changed their meaning since the nineteenth century – far from it. But I do want to say that, if they have, it might well be because the notion of empathy is more determinately or centrally located in our present notions of rightness and goodness than it was in earlier notions. And if the terms haven't changed meaning, what we have been saying suggests that it may be plausible to claim that the notion of empathy plays some sort of role within that unchanged meaning.

The above clears the way for a possible definition of moral words in terms of the notion of empathy. But at this point I have no idea how to produce one: one that is plausible as a definition and that helps us understand both why distinctions of empathy are morally relevant, and why empathy is so important to moral motivation (by which I mean not the motive to be moral, but rather, those motives, like caring for others, that morality approves of).[45] Of course, it

127

might be possible to offer an explanation of these things that *doesn't* appeal to a relevant definition of moral rightness and/or goodness, and I would now like to make a stab at doing just that.

If empathy were necessary to moral understanding, to an individual's understanding of, and ability to make, basic moral claims (call this the 'empathy/ understanding hypothesis'), then that would help to account for the wide correspondence between distinctions of empathy and the moral distinctions we want to make – and that I am assuming are valid. We have seen that empathy leads us to be more responsive, for example, to perceived pain than to pain we merely know about. But if our empathy and, in particular, our differential empathic tendencies also enter into our understanding of moral judgments or utterances, that would help to explain why we understand/judge an unwillingness to relieve pain we perceive to be morally worse than an unwillingness to relieve pain that is merely known about. And similarly in other cases. Putting the matter another way, if the very same empathy that leads us to respond differently to different kinds of situation enters into our understanding of and claims about what is morally better and worse, it is no wonder that there is a correspondence between our differential empathic tendencies and the moral distinctions we intuitively want to make. This isn't very specific, to be sure; but I do think it indicates how the truth of the empathy/understanding hypothesis would help explain why moral distinctions largely correspond to differences in our empathic tendencies. And it might also entail that, and help to explain why, moral judgments/utterances are intrinsically motivating.

But as I said, this is just a stab. It would be better if we had definitions or, failing that, at least a fuller account of how and why empathy is necessary to moral understanding (and judgment). But the small amount we have said may cast some further light on the question this conclusion began with – the question why distinctions of empathy so broadly mark the moral distinctions we intuitively want to make. That question presupposes what we have shown in the earlier chapters of this book – that distinctions of empathy *do* broadly mark the moral distinctions we intuitively want to make. Since it is difficult to believe that this correlation or correspondence is merely accidental, those earlier chapters make it reasonable to think that we can justify moral claims by reference to empathy. But the empathy/understanding hypothesis is supported by its ability to explain the correspondence we unearthed and discussed in previous chapters, and it can therefore serve to reinforce our confidence that empathy plays an important justificatory role within morality.[6]

Apart from meta-ethical issues of justification, the main purpose of the present work has been to improve on previous care-ethical accounts of morality. I have sought to do this, in the first instance, by using the notion of empathy to make and explain a number of important or central moral distinctions that care ethicists have not really or fully focused on: most especially deontological distinctions and other distinctions having to do with immediacy. But I have also sought to go beyond much of previous care ethics by offering a systematic account of both individual and political morality. Many previous care ethicists have left justice and rights largely to other, more traditional approaches, and they have often assumed that what the other approaches have to say complements, and can be harmonized or integrated with, care ethics. I argued in Chapter 5, however, that such a thing is not possible, that care ethics and traditional approaches like Kantian ethics or liberalism are actually inconsistent with one another and cannot, therefore, be harmonized or integrated.

That conclusion gives the care ethicist all the more reason to offer his or her own account of justice, respect for autonomy, and rights, to try to offer a comprehensive picture of moral values. And this is certainly something I have attempted (at least in sketch or outline) here. But perhaps at this point other care ethicists will see the possibility, and the necessity, of such a more systematic employment of care-ethical ideas. They might find the idea of empathy helpful to that enterprise, but they might also find ways of developing and expanding care ethics that this book in no way, or just partly, anticipates. Only time will tell.

Notes

1 Richard Holton and Rae Langton, 'Empathy and Animal Ethics' in Dale Jamieson, ed., *Singer and His Critics*, Oxford: Blackwell, 1999, esp. pp. 222ff.

2 Thomas Nagel, *The Possibility of Altruism*, Princeton, NJ: Princeton University Press, 1978; John McDowell, 'Virtue and Reason' in R. Crisp and M. Slote, eds, *Oxford Readings in Virtue Ethics*, Oxford: Oxford University Press, 1997.

3 Jeanette Kennett, 'Autism, Empathy, and Moral Agency', *Philosophical Quarterly* 52, 2002, pp. 340–57.

4 As Nel Noddings (*Caring: A Feminine Approach to Ethics and Moral Education*, Berkeley, CA: University of California Press, 1984) and many others have pointed out, caring about another person doesn't necessarily involve thinking about the moral status or moral nature of (one's) caring. The caring individual may be focused on the welfare of another person and not worried about whether what s/he does for that other person is morally right or obligatory.

5 In some previously published work, I sketched a way in which one might try to define moral concepts in terms of empathy, but I am no longer happy with those efforts.

6 Does my acceptance of the empathy/understanding hypothesis, and of the view that good actions reflect or express certain motives/feelings, commit me to non-cognitivism about moral language and therefore subject the present theory to all the problems that are known to beset non-cognitivism? I don't think so, but to prove as much would require a substantial discussion that would take us away from the main focus of this book. However, let me at least point out that there are a number of philosophers who treat sentimentalism as not necessarily committed to non-cognitivism: among them, David Wiggins, 'A Sensible Subjectivism' (in S. Darwall, A. Gibbard and P. Railton, eds, *Moral Discourse and Practice*, New York: Oxford University Press, 1987, pp. 237–42) and Stephen Darwall, *The British Moralists and the Internal 'Ought': 1640–1740* (Cambridge: Cambridge University Press, 1995, esp. pp. 214f.). Anyone who regards Hume as an ideal observer theorist also presumably regards sentimentalism as not entailing non-cognitivism.

INDEX

Related titles from Routledge

Ethics and the Limits of Philosophy
Bernard Williams

'Williams's discussions are much to be valued: his explicitness and argumentative ingenuity focus the issues more sharply, and at greater depth, than any comparable work I know ... One of the most interesting contributions of recent years, not only to ethics but to philosophy.'
John McDowell, Mind

'This is a superior book, glittering with intelligence and style.'
Thomas Nagel, Journal of Philosophy

'Remarkably lively and enjoyable ... It is a very rich book, containing excellent descriptions of a variety of moral theories, and innumerable and often witty observations on topics encountered on the way.'
Philippa Foot, Times Literary Supplement

By the time of his death in 2003, Bernard Williams was one of the greatest philosophers of his generation. *Ethics and the Limits of Philosophy* is not only widely acknowledged to be his most important book, but also hailed a contemporary classic of moral philosophy.

Presenting a sustained critique of moral theory from Kant onwards, Williams reorients ethical theory towards 'truth, truthfulness and the meaning of an individual life'. He explores and reflects upon the most difficult problems in contemporary philosophy and identifies new ideas about central issues such as relativism, objectivity and the possibility of ethical knowledge.

This edition includes a new commentary on the text by A.W.Moore, St. Hugh's College, Oxford.

ISBN 10: 0-415-39984-X (hbk)
ISBN 10: 0-415-39985-8 (pbk)
ISBN 10: 0-203-94573-5 (ebk)

ISBN 13: 978-0-415-39984-5 (hbk)
ISBN 13: 978-0-415-39985-2 (pbk)
ISBN 13: 978-0-203-94573-5 (ebk)

Available at all good bookshops
For ordering and further information please visit:
www.routledge.com

Related titles from Routledge

On Education

Harry Brighouse

'a rare example of a philosophical discourse with a direct relevance to contemporary policymaking ... If forthcoming debates about education policy do not draw heavily on what he has to say here, then they will be severely impoverished.' – *Julian Baggini, Times Educational Supplement*

'Clearheaded, acutely perceptive, and utterly lucid, this is the one book about education which *everyone* can and should make time to read.' *Randall Curren, University of Rochester, USA*

'This is a clearly structured and thought-out book ... It's polemical but also introduces the reader to key arguments and issues.' – *Stephen Law, Royal Institute of Philosophy*

What is education for? Should it produce workers or educate future citizens? Is there a place for faith schools – and should patriotism be taught?

In this compelling and controversial book, Harry Brighouse takes on all these urgent questions and more. He argues that children share four fundamental interests: the ability to make their own judgements about what values to adopt; acquiring the skills that will enable them to become economically self-sufficient as adults; being exposed to a range of activities and experiences that will enable them to flourish in their personal lives; and developing a sense of justice.

He criticises sharply those who place the interests of the economy before those of children, and assesses the arguments for and against the controversial issues of faith schools and the teaching of patriotism.

Clearly argued but provocative, *On Education* draws on recent examples from Britain and North America as well as famous thinkers on education such as Aristotle and John Locke. It is essential reading for anyone interested in the present state of education and its future.

ISBN 10: 0-415-32789-X (hbk)
ISBN 10: 0-415-32790-3 (pbk)
ISBN 10: 0-203-39074-1 (ebk)

ISBN 13: 978-0-415-32789-3 (hbk)
ISBN 13: 978-0-415-32790-9 (pbk)
ISBN 13: 978-0-203-39074-0 (ebk)

Available at all good bookshops
For ordering and further information please visit:
www.routledge.com